BRIGHT LIGHTS, BIG CITY

LONDON ENTERTAINED 1830–1950

Gavin Weightman

BRIGHT LIGHTS, BIG CITY

LONDON ENTERTAINED 1830–1950

C&B

COLLINS & BROWN

To Thomas Beaton Weightman

HALF-TITLE: *The exterior of the Oxford Music Hall around the turn of the century by Joseph Pennell*

TITLE PAGE: *An advertisement for one of the most popular forms of Victorian entertainment, the black minstrel, in 1885*

FRONT COVER: *London street scene by M. Grieffenhagen, 1926 (E T Archive)*

BACK COVER: *Programme for the Palace Theatre and cover for a Little Tich songsheet (Mander & Mitchenson Theatre Collection)*

First published in Great Britain in 1992
by Collins & Brown Limited
Mercury House
195 Knightsbridge
London SW7 1RE

British Library Cataloguing-in-Publication Data:
A catalogue record for this book
is available from the British Library.

ISBN 1 85585 131 8 (hardback edition)
ISBN 1 85585 144 X (paperback edition)

Conceived, edited and designed by Collins & Brown Limited
Editorial Director: Gabrielle Townsend
Editor: Sarah Hoggett
Picture Researcher: Philippa Lewis
Art Director: Roger Bristow
Designer: Bill Mason
Filmset by Tradespools Ltd., Frome
Reproduction by J. Films, Singapore
Printed and bound in Italy by New Interlitho SpA, Milan

CONTENTS

INTRODUCTION

THIS IS NOT A NOSTALGIC journey back to the foggy ruins of music hall, nor is it a celebration of London's theatrical heritage. It is more a history of popular entertainment on stage and screen, from the time London began to grow rapidly in the 1830s until the pleasure palaces, built in wave after wave during the following century, were for the most part abandoned, to lie in ruination until demolished or a new use found for them.

Today, London is both a mecca for theatre lovers from all over the English-speaking world and a veritable Pompeii of vanished pleasure resorts. What remains of West End theatreland – wonderfully rich though it is – is of small importance for Londoners themselves. Only about a third of tickets for West End shows are sold to Londoners: the West End has become a place to go for a special occasion. Even in the suburbs, where going to the theatre, the music hall and above all the cinema was once a routine part of life, for the great majority of people it is no longer so. Working-class theatre ended at the turn of the century; music hall vanished in the late 1950s; and cinema all but died in the 1970s.

Bright Lights, Big City, which accompanies London Weekend Television's six-part documentary series, delves into the gas-lit past to discover the forces that gave rise to new forms of metropolitan entertainment. What distinguished London in the Victorian and Edwardian periods was not so much a genius for *creating* new forms of entertainment, nor artistic inspiration, but the fact that it was a huge market place. It was the sheer size of its audience, with their growing spending power and increased leisure time, that gave rise to new forms of commercial showbusiness.

For those who got the formula right, huge profits could be made out of amusing Londoners. In an age when people's homes were often cold and miserable, providing warm and brilliantly lit surroundings was an essential part of the success of showbusiness, from the gin palaces of the 1830s to the super-cinemas of the 1930s. The greater part of what survives in the West End was built in the boom period for theatre and music hall from the 1890s to 1914. London's largest

theatre, now the home of the state-funded English National Opera, is the Coliseum, built for variety shows in 1904 by the showbusiness tycoon, Sir Oswald Stoll. As all the successful Victorian actor-managers recognized, however much they wanted to elevate the taste of their audience, they were, at the same time, in a commercial business. In London's West End today, the bulk of the most successful shows are musicals that run for years on end.

The kind of entertainment which was popular in the 'dream palaces' of the past does, to some extent, reflect the preoccupations of the day: the blood and thunder melodramas of East End theatres often dealt with the trials of London life, and the music halls satirized domestic matters in song. But what appealed to the audience was never *simply* a mirror of London life. From the very beginning the capital's 'dream palaces' drew in an international cast of talent: London was always an insatiable *market* for entertainment, rather than a creator and exporter of indigenous talent, though London stars, once their reputation was made, did find fame in Europe and America.

Though the Victorian showbusiness machine was driven by rampant commercialism, what it created was always the subject of critical concern by those who feared the potential power of 'the mob' and the twin evils of drink and sex, the spicy ingredients of so much popular entertainment. The moralists' own attempts to deflect the mass audience's interest away from what they regarded as corrupt were largely a failure. However, the culmination of a century of evolution in entertainment was a greater and greater 'respectability' on the part of the audience. In the end, moralists and money-makers went hand in hand.

One section of the London audience, broadly speaking the 'respectable' middle classes, had created for them in the latter part of the nineteenth century a new kind of theatre in which polite behaviour became *de rigueur*. This is essentially the West End theatre we know today – though habits are rapidly changing again – in which the playgoer dresses up, eats before or after the show, and does not drink during the performance as was the custom in music halls until the end of the century. The behaviour of audiences is an intriguing and often amusing subject.

As everyone knows, since the mid-1950s the popularity of television has devastated variety theatres and cinemas, with the result that popular *public* entertainment in its old form has vanished. Popular taste, much more fickle than that with pretentions to 'art', has

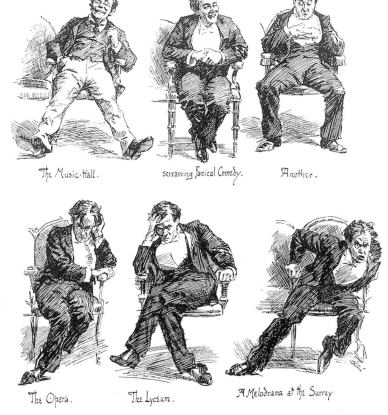

The Music-Hall.   Screaming Farcical Comedy.   Another.

The Opera.   The Lyceum.   A Melodrama at the Surrey

LEFT: *The arrival of early cinema shows – often as part of a music hall bill – rapidly changed the nature and experience of London entertainment. This postcard of the bioscope makes fun of the unaccustomed darkness of the auditorium in film shows.*

LEFT: *In the Victorian period audiences were very much divided by the kind of entertainment they went to see. This cartoon from* Punch *in 1894 gives a satirical – though not entirely far-fetched – description of the reaction of playgoers to high-brow and low-brow theatre.*

moved quickly with the times so that music hall, cinema and television have, as it were, gobbled each other up in turn leaving the abandoned Empire and the once thriving Roxy in the high street.

However, the London theatrical audience still plays a crucial part in judging new shows, as it has done throughout the period studied here. And that audience, which has always judged what it wants for itself, unconcerned by the dissenting voices of the critics, is the hero (and heroine) of this book. Wherever possible first-hand descriptions of its likes and dislikes and its experience of entertainment have been brought in to illuminate the history.

The thematic arrangement of the book will, it is hoped, point up some of the continuities in popular taste, as well as the turning points, while at the same time drawing together the inter-related histories of theatre, variety and cinema. The narrow spotlight, trained mostly on stage and screen, misses many popular pastimes, but will, it is hoped, illuminate that much better the histories it follows.

CHAPTER

1

DREAM PALACES

A VIVID EVOCATION OF THE EXCITEMENT of the theatre in one of the poorer districts of London in the 1830s can be found in the biography of John Hollingshead, who was born in 1827 and died in 1904 after an eventful life as a journalist and theatrical manager. Hollingshead spent his early years in Hoxton, just north of the City, and described himself as a 'street arab' of the better dressed kind. As a boy he played cricket on the greens that still marked the outskirts of London, and he describes a typical prank which gave him and his friends their first glimpses of real theatre. At Britannia Fields there was a theatre set in a garden, the Albert Saloon. The Albert was a minor and badly built affair, but it was an East End theatre none the less. In *My Lifetime* Hollingshead wrote:

> *In the intervals of cricket we (the boys of the period) had bored holes at the stage end of the structure with our stumps, and through these holes we could sniff the scent of the footlights – the indescribable bouquet of stage gas, orange peel, damp playbills and mouldy scenery, which suggests a playhouse and nothing else. More than this, we could hear the words of the play, the clash of swords, and the shrieks of heroines in distress.*

The Albert Saloon was one of a number of theatres in London's East End, playhouses that had been built on to public houses, putting on drama and variety turns with a good deal of singing. The most famous was the Grecian in the City Road (also known as the Eagle). Though none of these theatres was exactly palatial, modern forms of entertainment were just beginning to become established as London grew rapidly in the 1830s. The traditional fairs and summer pleasure gardens – semi-rural places of entertainment – were beginning to lose their attraction and were tolerated less and less as the bricks and mortar of the expanding city covered the fields.

It was from this period that the first of the new gas-lit 'gin palaces' were built, that new theatres were founded in the East End, and the first chorus of the music halls could be heard in the singing saloons. All these provided new forms of indoor entertainment in ever more

RIGHT: *The forerunner of the dream palace – open-air magic at Cremorne, one of London's fashionable pleasure gardens. By the late nineteenth century, all the pleasure gardens had gone.*

lavish surroundings, which contrasted with the squalor in which the majority of people lived. Hollingshead himself saw arise in his lifetime the most splendid music halls and variety theatres, and was in the 1860s stage director of one of the grandest, the Alhambra in Leicester Square. By the time of his death, the first cinemas had been built, films were shown in variety theatres and the East End theatres of his youth were in sad decline.

He did not live to see the last, and in many ways the most extraordinary, phase in a century of building 'dream palaces' for the people, the rise from the late 1920s of the super-cinemas, not just in London's West End but throughout the capital. Since the 1930s there has been no further evolution of the dream palace, for greater domestic comfort and television have kept people much more in their homes, and the building of places of entertainment has ceased to be big business in London.

A great many of the old theatres, music halls and super-cinemas have been returned to dust, and all those that survive from the nineteenth century have done so because some new use has been found for them at critical times in their history. Ballroom dancing kept Covent Garden Opera House going from the late 1920s until the end of the Second World War; the life of many music halls was prolonged by conversion in the Twenties or Thirties to a cinema; cinema buildings, in turn, have been saved by the introduction of bingo to the decaying art deco splendour of the old dream palace.

For those anxious to preserve the fabric of London's theatrical heritage, the loss of buildings is a tragedy. In social terms, however, this is not necessarily so. The conditions that created a demand for 'dream palaces' were grim indeed. In the 1830s, when London's water was hideously polluted and its slums cold, damp, dark and rat-infested, the warmth and glitter of the gin shop was luxury. When the streets were black with soot, ill-lit at night and filled with drabbly dressed millions, the dazzle of coloured costume in the yellow glare of footlights was magical. When families lived in single rooms without a kitchen and took their Sunday dinner to be cooked in the baker's oven, the warm and lively music hall with its gas chandeliers, and its tables groaning with pies and porter, was opulence. And in the Twenties and Thirties, when most people still had coal fires, the floor was covered with lino and only the very rich had servants, the centrally heated, thickly carpeted cinema with its obsequious uniformed staff was truly palatial and dream-like.

RIGHT: *A sketch by George Cruikshank – a temperance reformer – of the gin palace, the prototype of later and much grander dream palaces for the people. The barmaids and the bar counter were innovations of the 'fast' drink trade.*

Though the meaning of 'dream palace' changed with the successive improvements in social conditions, its evolution from gin shop to super-cinema can be seen as a century-long adjustment to the problems of surviving in a great city. Crammed together in the fuggy warmth, Londoners sheltered shoulder to shoulder from the harshness of urban life. The dream palaces provided an essential temporary escape until the majority were reasonably well housed, well fed and electrically heated: once radio and, above all, television provided 'piped' domestic entertainment, the 'dream palace' was replaced by the 'ideal home'.

Gin palaces

As rural life gave way to a more regimented, but better paid, better lit, and more sophisticated town life, new kinds of entertainment, new places in which to enjoy that entertainment, and new habits of going out inevitably evolved. All the while, a social division grew between the kind of places, amusements and behaviour that were acceptable to the majority of working people and what was acceptable to the industrious, but increasingly refined, professional classes. 'Respectability' was demanded in entertainment, just as it was in other spheres of Victorian life, and respectability, in turn, had a great deal to do with drink.

The publican is a key figure in the rise of popular entertainment in the nineteenth century, and the single most enduring resort of pleasure in London was – and is – the public house. Even today it continues to be a place where new theatres, revues and carbarets find a home and an audience.

When John Hollingshead was a boy, the first of a new kind of London drinking haunt was being built. By the standards of the late Victorian period these were unremarkable, but in the early 1830s they were called – usually by those who objected to them – 'gin palaces'. In *Sketches by Boz*, the young Charles Dickens describes such a place in 1836; and the contrast between the brilliance of the public house and its drab surroundings was to remain a consistent image of the dream palace, from the Victorian pub to the super-cinema:

THESE are the *Customers*, youthful and old,
That drink the strong drinks which are sold night and day
At the bar of the Gin-shop, so glittering and gay.

THIS is the *Gin-shop* all glittering and gay.

ABOVE: *Another Cruikshank sketch, from the* Band of Hope Review, *of the gin shop or palace which first appeared in the 1820s, enticing passing trade with its gas lamps and fancy window decoration.*

ABOVE: *From Pierce Egan's* Life in London, *published in 1820, the earliest painting of the gin palace which had begun to replace the old-style 'parlour' public house.*

. . . the gay building with the fantastically ornamental parapet, the illuminated clock, the plate-glass windows surrounded by stucco rosettes, and this profusion of gas lights in richly gilt burners, is perfectly dazzling when contrasted with the darkness and dirt we have just left. The interior is even gayer than the exterior. A bar of french-polished mahogany, elegantly carved, extends the whole width of the palace; and there are two side aisles of great casks, painted green and gold, enclosed within a light brass rail . . . Beyond the bar is a lofty and spacious saloon, full of the same enticing vessels, with a gallery running round it, equally well furnished . . . behind it are two showily dressed damsels with large necklaces . . .

It is not certain where or when the first gin palace was built, but there was undoubtedly a building boom in the 1830s and, to the dismay of Temperance reformers, gin, gas light and glitter began to appear all over London. A correspondent of the *Temperance Penny Magazine* in 1836 reported with horror on the gin palaces on the Ratcliffe Highway in East London:

> *. . . at one place I saw a revolving light with many burners playing most beautifully over the door of the painted charnel house: at another about fifty or sixty jets, in one lantern, were throwing out their capricious and fitful but brilliant gleams, as if from the branches of a shrub. And over the doors of a third house were no less than THREE enormous lamps with corresponding lights illuminating the whole street.*

These gin palaces, forerunners of the much grander and larger late Victorian pubs, burst brilliantly on to the London scene for a number of reasons. Duty on spirits was greatly reduced in 1825 as part of a wider enthusiasm for free trade, and official figures on consumption rose alarmingly. Whether or not much more was drunk than before 1825, when smuggled spirits and illegal 'duty-free' supplies were

ABOVE: *A classic coaching inn, the Oxford Arms in Warwick Lane in the City in 1875. The railways had made the long-distance stage coach redundant, and these inns went into decline. A number in central London were converted into music halls in the 1860s.*

LEFT: *A wonderful picture of the Vine Tavern, Mile End Road in Whitechapel, just before it was demolished in 1903. With its huge gas lamp it was a gin palace which had outlived its period.*

greater, nobody knows. But there was a panic about gin drinking and in 1830, partly to encourage drinkers to switch to ale, a Beer Act was passed which allowed anyone to set up an alehouse on payment of a small licence fee.

Even if there had been no change in the licensing laws, London's rapid growth in the nineteenth century would certainly have given rise to a new kind of public house. The traditional drinking places were not, for the most part, designed to cater for the urban crowds. There were inns, like the Boar and Castle in Oxford Street, which were stage coach termini, with stabling for horses, courtyards and rooms where people could stay the night. They served both food and drink. Most of the alehouses and the dram shops, however, did not serve food, and inside were parlours with no bar.

In their design, the gin palaces began to reflect their new function, providing a large space for 'perpendicular drinkers', London workers tramping home from their daily labours, commuters in need of 'fast' food and drink. The historian Brian Harrison has pointed out that the drinking places that arose in the rapidly expanding London of the mid-Victorian period lined the working-class commuter routes. By the end of the century, after building booms in the 1860s and 1890s, the number of pubs was staggering. On the Whitechapel Road in East London there were 48 drinking places in a one-mile stretch; along the Strand there were 46 in less than a mile. Publicans, concerned to find sites that would capture the largest numbers of passers-by, favoured street corners, railway stations, horse tram and bus termini, park entrances and any spot that attracted pleasure seekers.

Once established, the new pub – built larger in the 1860s and redesigned with huge mirrors, a central rather than a long bar, and segregated rooms – took on the function of a meeting place and, often, an entertainment centre. Amateur 'free and easies', singalongs and harmonic meetings drew in the customers. There was naturally fierce competition between publicans to find added attractions that could help business. The publican became a substantial figure, and with money borrowed from the big breweries in exchange for becoming a 'tied' house, had funds to re-build in an ever-more lavish style.

Rustic revels in retreat

At the time the gin palaces arose in the 1830s, a great many London pleasure resorts and amusements were going into decline. The same forces that gave rise to the public house undermined the traditional fairs, the tea-gardens and other open-air places of entertainment. The rapid expansion of London surrounded these semi-rural resorts with new suburbs; the air was blackened by smoke from homes and factories; pleasure had to go 'indoors'. Social sensibility, too, was changing as people lost their rustic roots. To Hollingshead's contemporaries in the 1830s the traditional Bartholomew Fair, held over three days in the autumn of each year on the site of what is now Smithfield meat market – 'that annual festival of mud, dung, and riot', as he called it in his memoirs – was already regarded as something of a public nuisance:

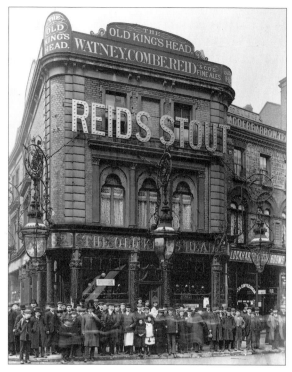

... This was the oddest combination of town and country ever brought together ... it combined the bustle, business and attractions of a cattle-market with a congress of peripatetic show-men ... Bulls that were occasionally mad, half-tortured sheep, dogs, drovers, and bulls that were perfectly sane on their way to be pole-axed in dirty slaughter-houses down back streets, were mixed up with prize-fighters, clowns, rope-dancers, fire eaters, city constables, butchers, salesmen, ginger-bread booths, thieves and parsons all crowding together, and wading through a London bog.

Although these shows were held on the site outside Bartholomew's Hospital only a few days a year, they travelled right round London, with their booth theatres, 'learned pigs', celebrated dwarfs, strong men and woman and all kinds of menageries and freak shows. The Easter Fair at Greenwich opened the season, then there was Deptford, Ealing Fairlop, Mitcham, Camberwell, Bartholomew, Enfield and finally Croydon. Each year there would be some spectacular novelty just arrived from Europe. A star turn in 1832 was part of the Italian conjuror Capell's show, a company of cats that beat a drum, turned a spit, ground knives, played the organ, hammered on an anvil, ground coffee and rang a bell. There was also a dog which challenged any man to a game of dominoes. Bartholomew Fair was still going strong in the 1830s. For a long time, however, there had been concern about the nuisance it caused, and bit by bit the City authorities closed it down,

ABOVE: *The Old Kings Head in the Euston Road in 1906. Above the huge gas lamps is an electric advertisement for Reid's Stout, and next door – to the right – Lockhart's Cocoa Rooms. Popular restaurants, serving cheap meals but no alcohol, were a challenge to publicans who smartened up their premises and provided partitioned bars to segregate the respectable from rougher clientele.*

until in the 1850s only a gingerbread man or two was left. It had gone entirely by 1855.

During the same period, the pleasure gardens that had been so popular in the eighteenth century began to lose their appeal. The most famous were Vauxhall and Ranelagh, but there were many others around London, including Sadler's Wells. A speciality of Vauxhall was its spectacular firework displays, and it was here in 1816 that Madame Saqui gave the first of many remarkable performances,

walking a tightrope tied to a sixty-foot-high post as fireworks crackled around her. It was just one of many spectacular shows put on in London's pleasure gardens.

A contemporary account is given by A. Thornton in *Don Juan in London*, published in 1836:

> ... the gardens are beautiful and extensive, and contain a variety of walks, brilliantly illuminated with variegated coloured lamps and terminated with transparent paintings, the whole disposed with so much taste and effect, as to produce sensation bordering on enchantment in the visitor ... the wonderful aerial ascent of Mme Saqui from the most astonishing height, on a tight rope; an exhibition that again transports the spectator in imagination to fairy land, since the ease, grace and rapidity, with which this lady descends, aided by the light of fireworks that encompass her, and still more by the darkness of the surrounding atmosphere, combine to give the appearance of flight of some celestial being ...

Though these spectacles continued to draw the crowds for some years to come, new and more purely metropolitan forms of entertainment – gin palaces, theatres and music halls – were arising, which in time absorbed much of the variety of acts of the fairs and pleasure gardens. Vauxhall Gardens closed in 1859. New pleasure gardens, such as Cremorne established in 1832, were successful for a time, but gradually

became unfashionable and closed either for lack of funds or because stricter licensing authorities refused to allow them. Cremorne was refused its licence in 1877.

The patent monopoly

The way in which popular entertainment had by then developed was governed to a considerable degree by a very strange and, by the 1830s, anachronistic set of laws. The first London theatres, in Shakespeare's day, had been to the east of the City, and later on the South Bank. But the theatrical world was devastated by Cromwell and the Puritans: playhouses were pulled down and actors branded as vagabonds. With the restoration of the monarchy under Charles II in 1660, a cautious return to licensing theatre had been made. Two members of the King's Household, Thomas Killigrew and Sir William Davenant, were given Patents which allowed them to form theatre companies to act Shakespeare and 'legitimate drama'. Though the meaning of this term was continually disputed, it generally meant Shakespeare, or the spoken word on stage *without* music. It did not include ballet or pantomime, which was mimed – a 'dumb show'. Killigrew built a new theatre in 1663, Drury Lane (a much more primitive and smaller building than stands there now); and Davenant formed a theatre in Lincoln's Inn Fields, the Patent for which was transferred over time and led to the building of the first Covent Garden in 1732.

For nearly two centuries this theatrical monopoly of straight drama, based on the often disputed Patents, inhibited the building of new theatres in London, although it by no means put a stop to it. The theory behind the Patents was that monopoly was a good thing, and would maintain standards, a political belief which Free Traders who came to the fore in the early 1800s bitterly opposed. Theatres without a Patent struggled against the law, ever ingenious in their efforts to present plays which – by the inclusion of music – could not be classed as 'legitimate'.

In 1737, the responsibility for licensing plays and theatres within Westminster and other places where there was a Royal residence passed to the Lord Chamberlain's office. Licences were awarded to theatres other than Drury Lane and Covent Garden, notably the Kings Theatre in the Haymarket and the Little Theatre almost opposite it. The Kings Theatre became known as the Opera House, and there was agreement that it would avoid competition with the Patents as far as drama went. The Little Theatre, built by a carpenter as a speculative

LEFT: *A typical bill of fare at a pleasure garden in 1824 – a programme of variety 'speciality' acts which ended up in music hall. There were many such gardens on the outskirts of London in the first half of the nineteenth century, most of them attached to pubs.*

RIGHT: *The actor John Palmer who, in the late eighteenth century, left Drury Lane and made a brave, but fruitless, attempt to establish a grand new theatre east of the City in defiance of Covent Garden and Drury Lane's monopoly on drama.*

venture in 1720, mostly got by in the summer months when Covent Garden and Drury Lane were closed. (It became the Theatre Royal, Haymarket, in 1766; Her Majesty's Theatre now stands on the site of the Opera House.) Even in the eighteenth century, there was a tremendous suppressed demand for drama in London, but whenever an actor or speculator with an interest in putting on plays tried to build a new theatre, the Patents objected and called in the law, which was always upheld. A great many troupes of players were, over the years, arrested and fined for daring to put on Shakespeare or other dramas in defiance of the Patent Theatres. It was a ludicrous state of affairs, in which all the theatres other than Covent Garden and Drury Lane were at the mercy of unfathomable rules.

There were many memorable battles in the fight to free the London stage of this absurd restriction. In the East End of London, new theatres were built in defiance of the law, their popularity established by enthusiastic patronage, before they were forced either to close down or to steer clear of drama. The greatest and most influential attempt to break the monopoly was made by a popular comedy actor, John Palmer, who had made a name for himself at Drury Lane and the Haymarket. He raised the money to build a new theatre at Wellclose Square, not far from the Ratcliffe Highway in East London, and called it, rather impudently, the Royalty. When this theatre was opened with great ceremony in 1787 it was judged by *Gentleman's Magazine* to be the finest in London at the time, with a seating capacity for 2,594.

Even before the curtain opened on the stage of the Royalty, the Patent Theatres had made their first thrust: the cast would be branded as vagrants and prosecuted. To avoid this Palmer made it a 'free' performance, giving all the proceeds to the London Hospital. Then he strode on to the boards and delivered the following rhyming riposte to his persecutors:

> *Yet some there are who would our scheme annoy;*
> *'Tis a monopoly they would enjoy.*
> *The Haymarket, Covent Garden, Drury Lane,*
> *Send forth their edicts;*
> *Three jarring States are leagu'd in jealous fit,*
> *And they – whom* wit *maintains –* wage war on wit.

A few hecklers in the audience were drowned by the cheers and, after playing Jacques in *As You Like It*, Palmer issued a final retort. He had, he said, obtained a local magistrate's licence which should be

good enough and, given the freedom others had to put on all kinds of mindless amusements, he should be allowed to play Shakespeare.

But Palmer did not dare risk the livelihood of his company after this bold speech. The theatre closed for two weeks, then re-opened without Shakespeare, which was replaced by a variety bill: dancers, pantomimes – acceptable because they were dumb shows – comical musical pieces called burlettas, and the like. The spies from the Patent Theatres, jealous of the Royalty Theatre's success with its variety show, watched closely lest something slip in which might be defined as drama – a ridiculous legal nicety, which rested on whether two characters on stage indulged in some kind of dialogue, without music. One night, in a mime act, one character inadvertently spoke to another: Palmer was arrested, convicted and allowed out on bail. He went back in the end to acting at Drury Lane and others took over the Royalty. Other theatres, in an effort to get round the Patents, accompanied Shakespeare with an occasional burst of music, but there was never any certainty that the law would accept the device.

By the 1820s, despite the Patent monopoly, East End theatres of various kinds were being established. By the standards of the day, these were lavish buildings. In 1828 the Pavilion Theatre was opened opposite the London Hospital in Shoreditch and boasted 'elegant and commodious boxes ... the Decorations and Embellishments are by the first masters. Centre Chandelier of beautifully Variegated Cut Glass designed and executed by Mr Simonds illuminated with splendid gas light.' Later rebuilt after a fire in 1856 it was called the 'Drury Lane of the East'. Another theatre with a brief but eventful life was the New City, founded in Milton Street (later Grub Street), which tried to evade the Patents by selling tickets not at a box office but in a clothes shop opposite, with the pretence that the performance was free. It opened around 1830, put on many melodramas and pantomimes and saw Edmund Kean play to thunderous applause. One of the leading actresses, Miss Smithson, later married the composer Hector Berlioz. But a series of managerial crises closed the City Theatre in 1836.

A year before the City closed, the Standard Theatre was opened by Britannia Fields, on a site which not long before had been the scene of wrestling matches. In its first years the Standard was part pleasure garden, part theatre. An advertisement of 1839 proclaimed:

The entertainments at this attractive place of amusement continue to give the most unbounded satisfaction; they comprise vocal and instrumental concerts, ballets, vaudeville ... Illuminations every evening, Grecian fountains, rustic alcoves and rural promenades. The first military band of the country is engaged for the favourite waltzes, quadrilles etc. of Strauss, Musard, Lanner and other talented composers of the day. Splendid fireworks etc. on gala nights. A well-attended ball on Saturday evening (ladies free), admission sixpence.

ABOVE: *The City of London Theatre in Bishopsgate Street was built in 1834, but not opened until 1837 because of difficulties in getting a licence. It then flourished as a classic popular theatre with melodramas and animal shows, which in one case included an 'intelligent elephant'. In the 1860s it went into decline and ended up as a temperance hall.*

The kind of drama the Standard put on was typified by *The Terror of the Mountains, or the Old Man of Lebanon*, a swashbuckling tale of the Crusaders with sword fights – always very popular – and a finale in which the entire back of the stage collapsed to depict the destruction of a towered fortress. In later years, after the inevitable burning down of the original building, the Standard became one of the most splendid theatres in the East End. But that was after the final round of the battle against the Patents had been fought. Still, in the late 1830s, troupes of actors were being arrested for playing drama. As a young boy, John Hollingshead was himself a victim. He liked to go to the little, make-shift theatres called 'penny gaffs' of which there were many in the East End. One night he was crammed in with other boys watching a performance of *Othello*, no doubt abbreviated and re-written from Shakespeare's original as most of the Bard's plays were at the time. The performance was raided by the police, and much later in his memoirs Hollingshead was still fuming with rage at the treatment the players and audience received.

> *Dog fights, rat fights, badger drawing, skittle-sharping, even Shove-halfpenny were more or less winked at; but Shakespeare – Shakespeare without a licence – Shakespeare in defiance of the patent houses, Drury Lane and Covent Garden – horrible! degrading! Everybody was very properly taken into custody. The actors in their paint, the fiddlers with their instruments of torture, the audience in their rags, the servants, the proprietor – some eighty people in all – were marched off to Worship Street [the police station].*

Hollingshead was given a box round the ears, but the others were fined. The absurdity of this kind of episode sooner or later would lead to a change in the law. The rising demand for theatre was being stifled. The situation had become all the more ridiculous when Covent Garden and Drury Lane were rebuilt after fires in the early 1800s: the new premises were so large that people complained they could not hear the drama in them. To make money the owners – the supposed upholders of national theatre – often took to putting on horse shows and a variety of other popular entertainments.

The last round in the battle against the Patents was fought out in Hoxton, East London. The Union Saloon in Shoreditch was one of a number of notable 'saloon theatres' in the 1830s, half theatre, half song and supper room. Sam Lane, a Devonshire lad come to London to make his fortune, worked at the Union, and later took it over. He put on a drama, the popular *Black Eyed Susan*, and was promptly arrested and fined and his theatre closed down for infringing the Patent rights. This was around 1840, and it caused a storm of protest.

According to A. E. Wilson in his book *East End Entertainment*, Sam Lane headed a march on Westminster, followed by his patrons carrying banners proclaiming 'Workers want theatres' and 'Freedom for the people's amusements'. Lane then took over the Britannia Saloon

ABOVE: *A comical view of a London 'penny gaff' in the 1870s by the French artist, Gustav Doré. There were hundreds of these cheap theatres in London in the nineteenth century, until most were closed down by the licensing authorities.*

in Hoxton, and set it up as a theatre in 1841. Hollingshead, who knew it then, describes it as more like a music hall than a theatre, but in time the New Britannia, known affectionately as the Brit to the locals who were its entire support, became one of the grandest and most valuable theatres in London.

But this was not until the passing of a critical piece of legislation, the Theatre Regulation Act of 1843, which acknowledged that the old monopoly was unworkable. Sam Lane's protest was the culmination of years of discontent. The 1843 Act finally abolished the Patent monopoly, and was a triumph for free traders. All manner of theatres could apply for a Lord Chamberlain's licence and put on drama unmolested, though the plays they put on had to be approved by the Lord Chamberlain. However, this Act, only five pages long, led to further confusion.

Pipes, porter, pies and plays

Since 1757, music and dancing licences had been issued by the justices, and comprised a different set of rules and regulations from the Lord Chamberlain's as applied to theatres. The latter was concerned with 'legitimate drama'; the former with the regulation of popular amusement and the local control of the places that provided it. After 1843, an enterprising publican like Sam Lane had a choice. He could either choose to put on drama, in which case he might be restricted in what the Lord Chamberlain would permit by way of refreshments in his theatre, or he could apply for a magistrate's licence and serve up whatever he wanted to his patrons, but he would not be allowed to play drama. By custom, rather than by law, it was not possible to hold both licences.

A great many historians attribute the rise of the music hall to this Act of 1843, for they say it forced publicans either to choose non-dramatic entertainment and go on allowing smoking, and serving drinks and food in the auditorium, or to abandon those very lucrative catering facilities in order to put on drama. In fact, the Act says nothing about the consumption of drink or food in theatres, and nobody is clear about what the Lord Chamberlain laid down by way of rules.

When examined by a Select Committee of the House of Commons in 1866, the representatives of the Lord Chamberlain's office were very hazy indeed about the application of any such rules. On the first day of the committee, the Right Hon. Spencer Cecil Brabazon Ponsonby of the Lord Chamberlain's office was cross-examined about drinking in

LEFT: *'Her first bouquet', a painting by Charles Green. A scene backstage at the Britannia Theatre, Hoxton, depicting, in the centre, the actor-managers Sam and Sara Lane, with performers. A man in the flies (top right) can be seen operating a limelight.*

theatres. He said if theatres applied for an excise licence they got it. The committee having been told by Ponsonby that music halls were essentially refreshment places and theatres places for playing drama, there followed this typical exchange:

MR LOCKE (*committee member*): *Are you aware that in many of those theatres there is a beer-engine in the pit, and likewise barrels of gin, brandy and all sorts of spirits, and that the privilege of selling those things is a very great source of profit to the managers?*
PONSONBY: *I cannot say I am aware of that. I know that the Excise Licence is granted under the Act of Parliament.*
LOCKE: *As a matter of course?*
PONSONBY: *Yes, as matter of course.*
LOCKE: *To that extent the theatres are as much public houses as music halls, are they not?*

RIGHT: *Although Hoxton's Britannia was chiefly a local theatre, its magnificent pantomimes attracted London-wide attention, and were even favourably reviewed by George Bernard Shaw, who was otherwise dismissive of popular theatrical entertainment in the late nineteenth century.*

FAR RIGHT: *A typical Britannia programme, combining variety acts and melodramatic plays. The nightly performances would start just before 7 p.m. and would go on until midnight with half-price admission for those arriving later in the evening.*

PONSONBY: Yes.

LOCKE: It only depends on the way in which the place is conducted?

PONSONBY: Yes; for by the Lord Chamberlain's regulations, the theatres are not allowed to sell spirits within the audience part of the theatre.

LOCKE: Are you quite sure of that?

PONSONBY: Yes.

LOCKE: Do you mean they are told that they have not that power?

PONSONBY: Under the rules of the Lord Chamberlain, spirits and refreshments are not allowed to be sold within the audience part of the theatre, excepting the people who walk up and down the pit with baskets.

And thus the cross-examination continues, with Ponsonby insisting that there *is* a distinction between serving drinks from baskets or at the back of the pit, and the alternative of sitting down to a full meal with alcoholic drink in the auditorium, as in a music hall. Mr Locke could find little difference. Later Ponsonby is asked if any music halls have applied for Lord Chamberlain's licences. They have, he says, but they would have to abide by the rules. These included no smoking in the auditorium, on the recommendation of several House of Commons committees, the last being in 1854. The applications, it appears, had all been withdrawn.

The strange thing is that after 1843, Sam Lane, and later his wife Sara, had a Lord Chamberlain's licence for the Britannia Theatre, Hoxton, yet all the descriptions of that theatre until the end of the century indicate that the audience smoked, ate and drank. Whereas the West End theatres in the second half of the nineteenth century did away with smoking and refreshment (see Chapter Four), the Britannia went on ignoring whatever rules there were. It seems probable that the Lord Chamberlain left the East End theatres alone.

H. G. Hibbert recalled the Britannia in the 1890s in *Fifty Years of a Londoner's Life*:

In the nineties what playgoer worth his salt would willingly miss the Britannia pantomime in which the septuagenarian Sara Lane would play the principal boy with all the bravery of tights and trunks to the delight of the gallery boys who worshipped her? Few restaurants got rid of so much solid food as the Britannia audience would consume during five or six hours dramatic debauch. Men walked to and fro incessantly with trays groaning beneath the

ABOVE: *A satirical, but in many ways evocatively accurate, picture of London theatre when drama was a very popular form of entertainment. This detail from a sketch by George Cruikshank shows the division between pit and box.*

*weight of pies in infinite variety, thick slices of bread plastered
with jam, chunks of cheese, slabby sandwiches, fried fish, jellied eels.
Gallons of ale washed down mountains of food.*

All this guzzling took place in what every commentator who ventured
East agreed was a splendid theatre, with an auditorium with a greater
capacity than either Drury Lane or Covent Garden. Charles Dickens
wrote of the Britannia in the *Uncommercial Traveller*:

*The object of my journey was theatrical, and within an hour I was
in an immense theatre, capable of holding 5,000 people. What
theatre? His Majesty's? Far better. Royal Italian Opera? Far supe-
rior to both for seeing in. To every part of this theatre are spacious
fireproof ways of ingress and egress. For every part of it convenient
places of refreshment and retiring rooms ... an unquestionable
humanising influence in all the social arrangements of the place
... The stage itself and all its appurtenances of machinery, cellar-
age, height and breadth, are on a scale more like the Scala at Milan
or the Grand Opera at Paris than any notion a stranger would be
likely to form of the Britannia Theatre, Hoxton ...*

The rise of the music hall

There really was no reason for theatres and music halls to develop sep-
arately, other than the vagueness of the 1843 Act and the dual licensing system. Either you had a music and dancing licence, or a Lord
Chamberlain's licence, but you could not have both because the rules
of the two licensing authorities differed, and they would not interfere
with each other. So even after the monopoly of the Patent Theatres
had ended, there were further battles between theatres and music
halls, especially in the West End, for the music halls wanted to put on
drama, but whenever they did they were liable to prosecution. As late
as 1911, the newly opened Palladium was fined for allowing an
excerpt from *Julius Caesar*.

Whereas few new theatres were founded in the decade after 1843 –
though many were re-built on a grander scale – the music halls arose
at an astonishing pace. There was no great difference between the prototype music halls that grew out of pubs and the popular saloon
theatres. Like the gin palaces that evolved into the much larger and
grander Victorian pubs, both saloon theatres and singing saloons gave
rise to much grander places by the end of the century, and there is no

doubt that it was the music hall, by then called a variety theatre, that became the dominant place for popular entertainment. There had been no music halls as such in the 1830s. By 1870 the *Era Almanack* could list 36 *large* halls in London alone. Very few, if any, of the entertainments provided by these popular palaces were new: all had been performed before somewhere in a singing saloon, a theatre, a pleasure garden, a fair or a circus. What was new was the way in which they were packaged by impresarios who recognized that there was a new market in a London population with a little more money and a little more leisure, and a taste for relatively refined surroundings and architectural razzamatazz.

The term 'music hall' was an old one, for there were many concert rooms in London, but it was given a new meaning in the 1850s. It was chosen deliberately to conjure up an air of respectability, for not all the forerunners of these new establishments were places of what came to be called 'family entertainment'.

A number of places compete for the honour of being the first ever of this new kind of music hall. The term appears to have been first used by the Surrey Music Hall, formerly the Grapes Tavern, in Blackfriars Road in the 1840s. But the story of the Canterbury Hall in Westminster Bridge Road, Lambeth, which in time became the most famous of Victorian music halls (Charlie Chaplin's father appeared there at the end of the nineteenth century), gives a clear indication of how tastes were changing.

In Shakespeare's day it had been a hostelry for pilgrims and took the name the Canterbury Arms after the abolition of the monasteries. It had long been known as a place of entertainment when it was taken over by a publican, Charles Morton, in 1848. Taking as his model the song and supper room Evans's, in Covent Garden, Morton built his first hall.

Evans's was housed in the basement of what had once been a Georgian hotel. It was founded by a Mr W. C. Evans, a chorister at nearby Covent Garden – a useful reminder that the antecedents of music hall were very widespread. He called it 'Evans' Late Joy's' (the building had originally been a hotel named Joy's). Evans's was for men only, and many lewd songs were sung as well as comic turns.

Evans retired, in 1844, handing over to another former chorister known as Paddy Green, who re-built the supper room and reformed the nature of the entertainment provided. Women were allowed to watch the entertainments, which included a choir of men and boys singing madrigals, ballads, and selections from operas, with piano or

RIGHT: *A programme for Evans's supper rooms in the 1850s. This basement hall in what had been a hotel in Covent Garden was the inspiration for the first music halls proper which began to be built in the 1850s and 1860s.*

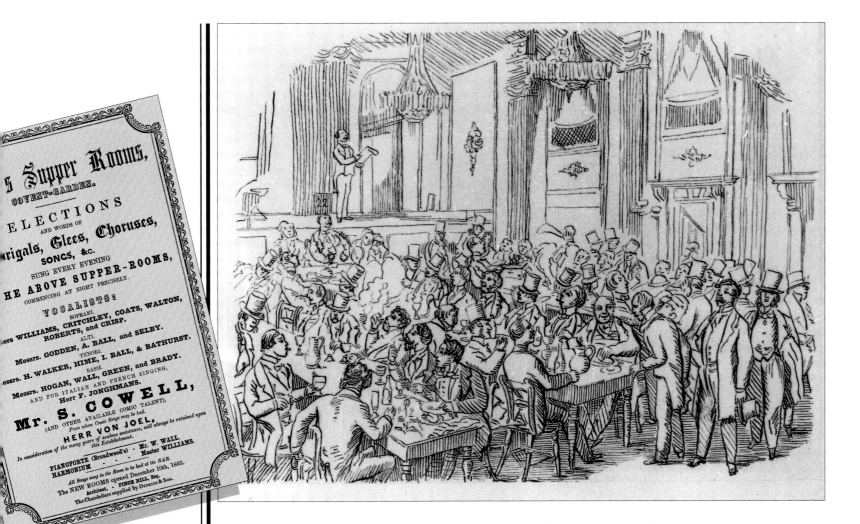

harmonium accompaniment, from an upper gallery if they were prepared to give their name and address – a protection against prostitution.

Evans's opened at 8pm, but did not really begin to hum until after midnight, when Paddy Green, snuff box in hand, officiated over a range of performances drawn from the best artists appearing at the pleasure gardens such as Vauxhall. Evans's was simply the most popular of a number of West End song and supper rooms, which included the Coal Hole in the Strand, the Cyder Cellars in Maiden Lane, Covent Garden (an American Fat Boy hamburger joint is now on the derelict site) and the Mogul in Drury Lane (site now of the New London Theatre). Outside

ABOVE: *A sketch which gives some idea of what Evans's was like, the person on stage – apparently number 22 on the bill – struggling to hold the attention of an audience heavily engaged in eating, drinking and talking.*

the central area were all the 'free and easies' in public houses, often with their pleasure gardens around, in which the drinking and jollity was encouraged with all kinds of comic turns and singalongs. With such a demand for entertainment, some of the best amateur performers were being encouraged by high fees to turn professional, and they would appear at many different places to earn their living.

Charles Morton was inspired by his enjoyment as a patron of Evans's to start up a small 'harmonic meeting' in a large back room of the Canterbury Arms. There was no admission charge, and a few professional paid singers performed alongside amateurs. Despite the fact that the 'harmonic meeting' was on Saturdays only, the early success of this venture – in the sale of drinks and food it encouraged – prompted Morton to build a larger hall. At the back of the Canterbury was an old skittle alley, a relic of the rural past of the area now swamped by the outgrowth of London. The new hall was up within a year, and seated 700 people. It had no stage but simply a platform for performers. Morton recreated some of the atmosphere of Evans's, paying some of the stars unprecedentedly high fees. It was not all vulgar fare, but included selections from opera, and the first performances of Offenbach in this country. Morton re-built again – in one week-end. Anxious not to lose custom, he had the new hall built over the old one without stopping the performances. One Saturday evening the skittle alley hall was demolished, and a new hall opened on the Monday.

ABOVE: *As Charles Morton's bold experiment in bringing in professional performers to his little music hall paid off, he rebuilt rapidly, finally opening the most spectacular place London had yet seen. Soon after this new hall was built, Morton moved into the West End, leaving the Canterbury to others.*

Morton had added a picture gallery which *Punch*, the satirical magazine, called 'The Royal Academy over the Water'. A description of the new hall is given in J. E. Richie's contemporary survey of the capital's amusements, *The Night Side of London*:

A well-lighted entrance attached to a public house indicates that we have reached our destination. We proceed up a few stairs, along a passage lined with handsome engravings, to a bar, where we pay sixpence if we take a seat in the body of the hall, and ninepence if we ascend into the galley. We make our way leisurely along the floor of the hall, which is well lighted, and capable of holding 1,500 people. A balcony extends round the room in the form of a horse-shoe. At the opposite end to that at which we enter is the platform, on which are placed a grand piano and a harmonium on which the performers play in the intervals when the previous singers have left the stage. The chairman sits just beneath them. It is dull work to him, but there he must sit drinking and smoking cigars from seven to twelve o'clock. The room is crowded, and almost every gentleman has a pipe or cigar in his mouth. Evidently the majority present are respectable mechanics or small tradesmen with their wives and daughters and sweethearts. Now and then you see a midshipman, or a few fast clerks and warehousemen. Everyone is smoking, and everyone has a glass before him; but the class that come here are economical and chiefly confine themselves to pipes and porter.

This new hall had been opened on 21 December 1856, and it drew a good deal of comment in the Press, which was struck by the refinement of the performances, the presence of women and the splendid surroundings. The Picture Gallery, which was open day and night, attracted favourable comment, and was regarded as a novel and 'improving' place in which to eat jacket potatoes and oysters washed down with porter.

At this time new music halls, not necessarily on the lines of the Canterbury, were springing up on the sites of old singing saloons in many parts of London. The entertainment was a movable feast – the same stars could do the rounds – and it was in the comfort and lavishness of the surroundings that the new impresarios competed. They came to draw more and more of their profits from the entrance fee, though the sale of drink and food remained important and was one reason why music halls were generally more profitable – and thus attracted greater investment – than theatres.

The kind of variety show that evolved, and the style of building that accommodated it, also answered the needs of the majority of Londoners more readily than the theatres. Much more is said about this in Chapter Four, but it is useful to note here that while middle-class theatre evolved to provide a single performance of a play, instead of various pieces as had been the style earlier, music hall offered variety. This meant that you could go in at any time, watch the pieces that amused you, and wander out again into the promenades which music hall proprietors soon learned to provide in the halls built after the

BELOW: *A sketch by a French artist of the typical chairman of the early music halls, often the publican himself who urged his customers to drink up and kept unwanted amateur talent off the stage. In the later, more sophisticated, music halls each 'turn' was numbered and the order of performance marked on a programme.*

Follies of the Day

ABOVE: *A poster for a melodrama, performed in a theatre but set in a music hall, a vivid illustration of the contrast between the two principal forms of entertainment in the Victorian era.*

RIGHT: *A song cover for the first super-star of modern entertainment, George Leybourne, who was born in the North East but brought up in London. He wrote many hits which he performed himself in flamboyant style, including 'The daring young man on the flying trapeze'.*

1860s. A chairman introducing the pieces gave way to a programme with the various 'turns' numbered, and the order of appearance indicated on the side of the stage. The potential profits of this kind of variety were quickly understood. At the same time as Morton was creating his 'palace' in Lambeth, the old Mogul Saloon in Drury Lane was turned into the Middlesex Music Hall (1851); the Mahogany Bar, on the site of the Royalty and Brunswick theatres in Wellclose Square in the East End, became Wilton's in 1856. In the 1860s were founded the Bedford in Camden Town, the Royal Standard Music Hall in Pimlico, Deacon's in Clerkenwell (1862), Collins, Islington (1862), which survived until the 1950s and is still remembered by many people, and the Metropolitan, Edgware Road, the last to disappear in 1962.

In 1857, the music halls began to invade the West End. The first was Weston's in Holborn on the site of the Seven Tankards and Punch Bowl Tavern, the success of which encouraged Charles Morton to look for his own West End site. He found the old coaching inn, the Boar and Castle in Oxford Street, at the junction with Tottenham Court Road, long obsolete since the coming of the railways, but still with its old courtyard which was relatively easily converted into a music hall. Renamed the Oxford, Morton's new hall opened in 1861, and the first London Pavilion, on the site of another old coaching inn, was founded in the same year.

A clear architectural style was evolving. All halls promised fine entertainment and good refreshments in the most modern and salubrious surroundings. Frequently they were burned down (this happened twice to the Oxford before it was ten years old) or pulled down, and each re-building was on a more magnificent scale. All the famous halls were re-built, often by new syndicates which moved in to run them. From 1862 funds could be raised from investors and the halls run as limited liability companies, which pumped more and more money into building and refurbishment. Specialist architects, the most celebrated being Frank Matcham whose name and stamp are on many of the finer halls built towards the end of the century, developed a baroque theatrical style. Music halls became finer than most West End theatres, and generally much larger. Where grand theatres were built, they tended to fail, and to become variety theatres. This was the case with the Palace Theatre in Cambridge Circus, which opened as the English Opera House in 1891 but soon became the Palace Theatre of Varieties.

By the 1880s, variety theatres were leaving behind their antecedents in the singing saloons. The change came with the building of

the new London Pavilion in 1885. As Charles Stuart and A. J. Park described it in their classic *The Variety Stage* of 1895:

> *Hitherto the halls had borne unmistakable evidence of their origin, but the last vestiges of their old connections were now thrown aside, and they emerged in all the splendour of their new-born glory. The highest efforts of the architect, the designer and the decorator were enlisted in their service, and the gaudy and tawdry music hall of the past gave place to the resplendent 'theatre of varieties' of the present day, with its classic exterior of marble and freestone, its lavishly appointed auditorium and its elegant and luxurious foyers and promenades brilliantly illuminated by myriad electric lights.*

The authors go on to say that these had been originally 'palaces' for the people, but they were now attracting some of the upper crust in the West End. In fact, the earlier buildings now appeared cheap and second-rate: the palace of 1861, unless it was rebuilt, was the flea-pit of 1891.

The final break with the past came when the Pavilion was taken over by the Syndicate Halls Company, and the old dining area was removed in 1881 and replaced with fixed seating. On the back of the seats were little trellised metal ledges for holding drinks. Again in 1900 it was given a new interior with a sloping or 'raked' auditorium, and was much like a very grand theatre – though in the vast range of entertainment it could choose to put on, from performing dogs to tightrope walkers, drama was still banned.

In 1904, the ultimate theatre of varieties was built close to Charing Cross at the bottom of St Martins Lane. This was a great monument to one of the new breed of variety entrepreneurs of the late Victorian period, Oswald Stoll, born in Australia and founder of many provincial music halls before he came to London. The story goes that Stoll watched the pedestrian traffic in the centre of London and noted the great crowds along the Strand, and looked for a site which would be close to the centre of this mêlée.

The Coliseum, created by Stoll and the architect Frank Matcham, is still there, though not quite in its original form. Apart from its size and splendour, with a specially built Royal Box connected to the street by a small tramway (which failed to work when Edward VII climbed inside it), Stoll introduced a vast revolving stage. In the opening weeks, he staged a re-run of the Derby, with live horses and jockeys galloping against the spin of the revolve, which could hit 20 miles an hour. It was also used to set up several scenes at a time, so that when one 'turn' was over the stage would spin to reveal the next act, a device which was not only the ultimate expression of theatrical presentation of variety but the setting for a good deal of unintended humour. On one occasion, according to Felix Barker, the biographer of the Coliseum, in *The House that Stoll Built*, a stage actress named Irene Vanburgh insisted against the advice of her agent on appearing at the Coliseum – a touch of class that was the kind of thing Stoll encouraged. She gave her rendition, left the revolving stage, and then returned to take a bow. In the meantime, however, the show had moved on and the next act involving two gorillas had swung into place. As she fled to her dressing room another star of the show, an intelligent elephant, picked her pocket.

At the start of the twentieth century, variety had become the dominant form of popular entertainment in London, and many theatres were converted into the new kind of music hall. But popular taste was changing, and there were new attractions in London. The very last of the grand variety theatres to be built was the Palladium, later to become synonymous with variety on television. This was opened on 26 December 1910 on the site of Hengler's Circus in Little Argyll Street.

Old-time music hall held what was to be its grand finale with the first ever Royal Variety Command Performance at the Palace Theatre in 1912. In the celebrated words of Oswald Stoll, who along with other impresarios and variety artists was later knighted, 'The Cinderella of the Arts has gone to the ball'. Notoriously, the greatest star of the day, Marie Lloyd, was not invited, perhaps for fear she would let the side down with a bit of her subtle vulgarity and because of her scandalous private life. It was a gesture which indicated more clearly than anything else that music hall had achieved respectability. In doing so it had abandoned its former vigour, and was in its death throes.

Cathedrals of the movies

Even before the Cinderella of the arts had gone to the ball, a new kind of dream palace was being built in London to house an entirely novel

LEFT: *The Palace Theatre in Cambridge Circus was built not as the plush music hall it became, but as The Royal English Opera House, the creation of Richard D'Oyly Carte. After the opening with a Sullivan opera in 1891, it failed, and it was sold to a company which made it into a variety theatre in 1892, with the veteran of the Canterbury, Charles Morton, later brought in to supervise the entertainment.*

RIGHT: *Glamorous girls and lavish surroundings brought the upper crust to variety at the Palace in the 1890s when music hall was becoming 'respectable'.*

form of entertainment – the cinema. It is always amusing to study the history of a new invention which becomes commonplace, and to learn how little its true potential was recognized at the time. But it is a puzzle why the showing of short, silent films about practically nothing should have captured the imagination of a public which had as an alternative splendid theatres and star performers not only in the

West End, but in the suburbs as well. There have been a number of attempts to explain how this came about, and why it was that the Victorian and Edwardian dream palaces, developed to entice their audiences as much by their architectural splendour as by their entertainments, failed in the face of competition from the flickering screen.

It has been argued that the public were, in a sense, ready for films, for throughout the Victorian period they had been slowly accustomed to all kinds of wonderful visual representations. There was the diorama, in which ingenious lighting effects brought alive dramatic scenes. This had arrived with the Frenchman and photographic pioneer, Louis Daguerre in the 1840s. Along with the panorama, a great circular picture depicting all kinds of events and wonders of the world, and later the great popularity of stills photography, the diorama had created an appetite for the kind of realism that only films could provide.

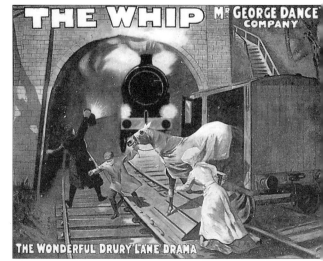

The first moving films were developed in the 1890s, and were at first 'peep' shows as there were no projectors. Here again, there was a long tradition of people peering into a lighted box to see amazing images: early lantern slide peep shows were a popular novelty even before the demise of Bartholomew Fair. Indeed, in the very early days of the Kinetescope produced by Thomas Edison, the American inventor, it was the showmen of the surviving London Fairs who became the chief film distributors. Later, with projection, the pioneers of film took their few, short movies to the variety theatres where they became just one variety act amongst many. Both the Empire and the Alhambra, Leicester Square were showing films in the 1890s.

Outside the variety theatres, the first places to charge admission to see films were the 'penny gaffs' – a term taken from the rough, illegal theatres in the Victorian period and applied to the first primitive cinemas – converted shops or any premises that would provide a few chairs and a screen. The first purpose-built cinemas – small and unelaborate compared with the great music halls – were being constructed in the early 1900s. The archaeology of early cinemas is fraught with difficulty because so few survive. But according to David Atwell in *Cathedrals of the Movies*, London's – and Britain's – first purpose-built cinema was the Biograph in Wilton Road, Victoria, opened

ABOVE: *Drury Lane became famous at the end of the nineteenth century for its 'sensational' dramas, of which one of the most spectacular was* The Whip *in which, under the direction of 'Sensation Smith', a train crash took place on stage. It was the ultimate in theatrical realism. Cinema soon stole Drury Lane's thunder.*

by an American, George Washington Grant, in 1905. Nothing much survives of its interior, but miraculously the decor of the Electric cinema in the Portobello Road, built in 1910, is almost untouched behind a much changed façade. The first West End cinema was the New Egyptian Hall in Piccadilly opened in December 1907, followed by the Electric Palace in Oxford Street (1908). After the passing of the Cinematograph Act of 1909, which licensed this new form of entertainment, cinemas sprang up all over London. Before the Great War, 500–600 seater cinemas were being built, and in May 1914 the Marble Arch Pavilion was opened with seating for 1,189, mostly on a single raked floor with a few boxes. A tea-room was attached. Perhaps the first cinema to call itself Super in London was opened in August 1916 on the site of the former Pyke's Cambridge Circus cinematograph Theatre of 1911.

Oswald Stoll, founder of the Coliseum, was already into cinemas in 1915, outbuilding everyone with the Stoll Picture Theatre, Kingsway, forged from the defunct London Opera House. (The mortality rate of opera houses without benefit of public subsidy appears to be around 100 per cent.) Among the finest pre-Great War cinemas were the Hackney Pavilion opened in 1913, the Odeon in Upper Street, Islington and the Astoria, Forest Hill. All have disappeared.

ABOVE: *Oswald Stoll, founder of the Coliseum, who turned to the new business of cinema-building with characteristic vigour and enthusiasm.*

RIGHT: *Early films were shown in fairgrounds and at music halls at the end of the nineteenth century, both the Empire and Alhambra, Leicester Square putting bioscope shows on the bill. The Egyptian Hall – also in Leicester Square – advertised the mutagraph, a rival version of the bioscope.*

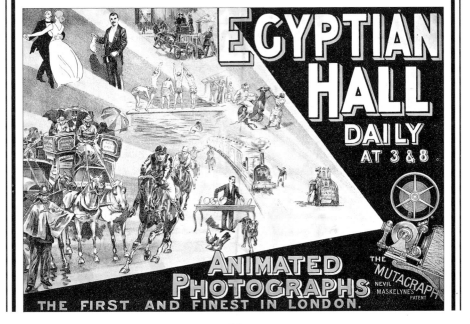

In the 1920s, the luxury of cinemas outshone any pre-war buildings and even Stoll was eclipsed. Though there had been 500 cinemas in London in 1912, the real boom was yet to come. The arrival of the 'talkies' in 1928–9 caused a sensation and a new round of cinema-building, and the creation of the 'Supers' with their programmes of four or more hours, in lavish surroundings, their cinema organs (the Wurlitzer and Comptons were invented to accompany silent films) and singalongs and their variety shows. The first casualty of the growing popularity of film, in the early 1900s, had been the old East End theatres, which were still drawing the crowds with their menu of farce and melodrama. Early films picked up exactly where this kind of drama had left off: many of the early silents were simply filmed versions of popular stage plays. Variety theatres at first absorbed films on to the bill, but even before 1914 one or two had been converted into cinemas. The Balham Empire Music Hall built in 1900 was the Balham Empire by 1907, showing only films. The Palaseum in Commercial Road, Whitechapel, which opened as Fienman's Yiddish Theatre in March 1912, became a cinema within a few weeks. And the Islington

BELOW: *The fashionable Empire, Leicester Square, in its Edwardian heyday. By 1925 it had been bought by Metro-Goldwyn and was converted into a super-cinema, with variety acts between the feature films.*

Palace, in Upper Street, was first a concert room of the 1860s, then the home of the Mohawk Minstrels, in 1902 a music hall, and the Blue Hall cinema by 1908.

In the West End one of the first and most spectacular conversions was of the Empire Music Hall into the Empire Cinema, Leicester Square. Built in 1882 the old music hall was bought by Metro-Goldwyn, the film distributors, and closed down in 1925. It was re-opened as a cinema in 1928 with seating for more than 3,000. Its splendid interior, with marble staircase in the foyer, walnut panelled walls, huge mirrors and crystal chandeliers, survived until 1961, when it was re-built.

The heyday of the super-cinemas, with their fantastic interiors, their uniformed staff, their organs rising from the pit glittering with

Souvenir

Gaumont

ABOVE: *The heyday of cine-variety in the ultimate dream palaces built between the wars. This is the Gaumont, Holloway. Every district of London had its super-cinemas, with stage shows as well as films.*

lights, their fully equipped stages and their elegant cafés, was in the 1930s. Going to the cinema became far and away the most popular form of entertainment of the day. It was a social event, and the ambience of the place, the undreamed-of, centrally-heated luxury, was as much an attraction as the films that were shown. John Huntley, who now runs an extensive film archive, recalls the atmosphere that prevailed in the late 1930s:

I think it is very difficult really to realize how marvellous it was in the 1930s to enter one of these wonderful Picture Palaces. The home in those day was a pretty bleak place – no central heating, a fire probably just in one room which created more draughts than it actually warmed you up – and suddenly in this luxurious setting of the cinema you were warm and there was a lovely deep carpet and you sank into a very comfortable seat which was such a contrast from the wooden seats you probably had in the kitchen in those days. And everybody was so polite to you, and even when I was 14 I well remember having paid my 6d, I was called 'Sir' by the staff and escorted to my seat. We used to go in about 12 noon and not come out till 8.00 in the evening and that was a day when you looked forward to not just seeing entertainment on the screen but sheer living luxury in total contrast to what it felt like at home.

Denis Norden, who was to become a successful comedy writer and TV presenter, was a very young cinema manager at the outbreak of the Second World War:

The loos were all marble. People were very impressed by something like that. The amount of indoor loos at that time was very much less than now so never mind having an indoor loo, having a MARBLE indoor loo was like going in Kubla Khan's palace. At the Trocadero, Elephant and Castle, I had 122 staff, so it was very labour-intensive and they were there to look after you. All the male staff at the Empire, Leicester Square, would line up before the doors opened and they would be given cigars and would puff the smoke. Now a cigar was something that if you were lucky you had at Christmas, so to come into a cigar aroma set the feeling immediately! As a manager it was your job to foster a feeling of luxury and never to lose it.

In those days you never saw white on the screen. You closed the curtains and put the footlights on blue and green and red and so on and you made sure that the censor's title hit the outside of the

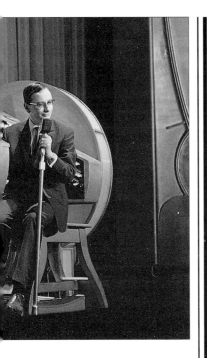

ABOVE: *The cinema organ was evolved to accompany silent films and was equipped with a range of sound effects, but survived to symbolize cine-variety in the days of the talkies. This is the organ at the Odeon, Leicester Square.*

curtains and then they parted. You fostered the illusion the whole time so that people in those days came out of the cinema with that kind of entranced look.

The big cinemas offered a variety of entertainments, absorbing the old into the new, just as the first music halls had drawn their acts from the disappearing pleasure gardens, fairgrounds and 'free and easy' saloons of the early nineteenth century. Audiences felt they were experiencing something excitingly new. In many ways they were, but they were also enjoying the last phase in the astonishing development of London entertainment. Many of the old variety acts ended their days on the stages of the super-cinemas: acrobats, trick cyclists, comic singers and even circuses played their part in a four-hour programme which included two feature films, cartoons, the electric organ and the news. The super-cinemas were also the last places (until some recent revivals) in which audiences might join in a singalong, as the organist rose from the depths beneath the stage fingering tiers of ivories as the words of popular songs were projected on the screen.

From the warm glow of the gin palace to the neon splendour of the Odeons and Empires, there had been a common and repeated theme of providing palatial surroundings for the people. In the late 1930s, a new invention appeared and was first seen in the surviving 'dream palaces' of the past, just as the bioscope had appeared, innocently enough, in the music halls. Quite a number of Londoners got their first glimpse of television in a pub. There was not much on show in 1936 or 1937, and nobody thought much of it. Cinema attendance peaked in 1946 in the period of austerity after the Second World War, when people had money to spend but not many goods to spend it on. But the cinema's heyday was already over: the thirties had been not the beginning of a new phase of building palaces for the people, but the end of an era.

In one century, thousands of buildings had arisen in London of which only a fraction remain, many of them recognized now only by the dedicated bands of enthusiasts who have tracked down their past. But they were, of course, simply buildings, and as the account of their rise and fall has made clear, what went on in them was wonderfully varied. All of them were built and run by people anxious to make money by creating or keeping up with popular taste. In showbusiness, there has never been anything more exciting, or soul-destroying, than trying to judge what novelty will appeal to the great London public.

ABOVE: *The dawn of a new era: the greatest of all variety theatres, the Coliseum, advertising tele-variety in 1935.*

CHAPTER

'A LITTLE OF WHAT YOU FANCY...'

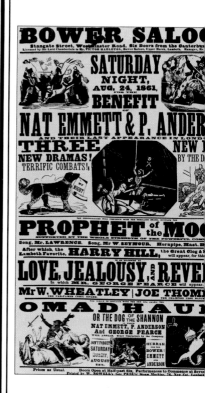

IN HIS ACCOUNT OF COSTERMONGERS' AMUSEMENTS in *London Labour & the London Poor*, first published in 1861, Henry Mayhew describes the rich street life of these archetypical, south-of-the-Thames Londoners, their sports and amusements. They go to the beer shop a good deal where they discuss business in their own back-slang, play shove-halfpenny and enjoy boxing. Not much time is spent at home. The better-off costermongers, Mayhew reckons, would make on average three trips a week to the theatre to see plays or concerts, almost always to one of their local playhouses, the Surrey, the Victoria, the Bower Saloon and (less frequently) Astley's. Mayhew records the account one costermonger gave of his tastes in entertainment – 'an intelligent and relatively well-educated man', he says.

Love and murder suits us best sir; but within these few years I think there's a great deal more liking for deep tragedies among us. They set men a' thinking but then we all consider them too long. Of Hamlet we can make neither end nor side; and nine out of ten of us – ay far more than that – would like it to be confined to the ghost scenes, and the funeral, and the killing off at the last. Macbeth would be better liked, if it was only the witches and the fighting. The high words in a tragedy we call jaw-breakers, and say we can't tumble to that barrikin. We always stay to the last, because we've paid for it all, or very few costers would see a tragedy out if any money was returned to those leaving after two or three acts. We are fond of music. Nigger music was very much liked among us, but it's stale now. Flash songs are liked, and sailor's songs and patriotic songs.

Here, recorded faithfully by Mayhew in the New Cut, Lambeth, is popular taste in a working-class area of London around the mid-nineteenth century.

This first-hand account is a reminder that the range of amusements the mass of Londoners have enjoyed since the early nineteenth century cannot be neatly described or compartmentalized, and the widespread belief that it was music hall that was the only crowd-puller is

LEFT: *A bill poster for the Bower Saloon in Lambeth in 1861. The Bower was a local theatre popular with the costermongers interviewed about their tastes in entertainment by Henry Mayhew. Dog dramas, in which canine heroes were the stars, were a speciality of the Bower.*

RIGHT: *The most celebrated star of music hall in its heyday, Marie Lloyd, has left little evidence of her undoubted talent. Her sound recordings are bad, and she died in 1922, at the age of 52, before sound film was generally available. Controversy still rages over how 'rude' she really was on stage.*

The Theatrical and Music Hall singing rights of this Song are reserved. For permissions apply to Miss Marie Lloyd.

THAT·WAS·A·BLOOMER·

"HE'D FORGOT TO TAKE THE TICKET OFF THE BLESSED BASSINETTE"

FIRST CHORUS.

That was a Bloomer—enough to make you laugh,
A Bloomer—upon my word, not half,
And when we'd left the tunnel and were going,
Cousin Johnny murmur'd in a tone, well, not polite,
"That was a Bloomer—a Bloomer!

Written by
HARRY·CASTLING,
Composed by
GEORGE·LE·BRUNN,
Sung by
MISS·MARIE·LLOYD.

quite wrong. There was just as much enthusiasm for melodrama as there was for the programme of comic songs, sketches, absurd speciality acts, trapeze artists, contortionists and performing dogs of music halls and later variety theatres.

To have any understanding of their appeal, however, involves a mental exercise in time travel which it is hard – if not impossible – to make. Old jokes and plots, tricks and favourite songs, for the most part strike a modern audience as lamentably lame and banal. As Michael R. Booth says in his classic study *English Melodrama*:

To recreate vanished playhouses, to populate them once again with noisy audiences, and to light them with flickering candles, harsh hissing gas, and soft multi-coloured pools of limelight, picking out actors long forgotten, acting in old-fashioned ways in front of creaking flats and jerking wings, is to make dead eyes see and dead ears hear.

Even more difficult is the question of why some forms of entertainment appeal to large audiences at particular periods, and what – if anything – they reflect of people's lives.

It is obvious that successful forms of entertainment must mean something to an audience: they must hit a nerve, strike a chord or tickle a fancy. Since the early nineteenth century an astonishing variety of performances has found favour with Londoners, from the last days of Bartholomew Fair, through the thrill of the American movies of the Thirties, to the theatrical musicals of today and the wide spectrum of entertainment on television. In some instances, especially with music-hall songs which deal with familiar domestic problems, it is easy to understand the way in which the stage reflects ordinary preoccupations and allows them to be re-lived in a humorous way. There are also, as we will see, many forms of popular entertainment the meaning of which is hard to interpret. It is not possible to make sense of it all, but from time to time the echo of applause in the great auditoria of the metropolis gives some clues as to the nature of London life and the way it has changed.

One great source of confusion about the relative popularity of drama and lighter kinds of entertainment in the Victorian period is the artificial division that grew up between theatres and music halls. The Theatre Regulation Act of 1843, which broke the monopoly on drama held by Covent Garden and Drury Lane, created in time a kind of apartheid of amusement. Because it was not possible to hold at one

and the same time a Lord Chamberlain's licence to stage drama, and a magistrate's licence to put on music and dancing, melodrama was excluded from the music halls.

At the time there was a great debate about the wisdom of this and a 1866 Select Committee of the House of Commons looked into the matter. While many witnesses regarded music hall as 'low', there were others of equal distinction who took quite the opposite view. Music hall had introduced a wide section of Londoners to refined amusement in the form of opera, ballet and madrigals, and had encouraged them to take a greater interest in the theatre. Contradictory evidence was brought forward, some saying the music halls were stealing the gallery audience from the theatres, others saying the opposite. But what was clear was that theatre and music halls were in fierce competition. Music hall managers had not turned their back on drama: they wanted to put it on. The problem was that when they did, they were liable to prosecution, and a complaint from a theatre that they were operating outside the terms of their licence would ensure a hefty fine.

A witness who gave evidence at the 1866 Select Committee was the immensely successful author of many Victorian melodramas, Dion Boucicault:

> *Twenty-five years ago the amusement-seeking public, so to speak, were divided into two classes; the upper classes which went to the theatres exclusively, and the lower classes which attended public houses and tea gardens and things of that kind; the music hall was the stepping stone between the two things. The artisan who used to go alone to the public house was induced by his wife, I presume, to go rather to the music hall, where he has something of the public house mixed with a little intellectual entertainment ... the large sums of money which have been made by managers in pits and galleries of theatres lately has been principally due to the pits and galleries of the theatres being recruited from the music halls.*

Although managers of theatres appeared to contradict Boucicault, saying that the music halls had taken away their gallery audiences, the essential point is that at this time audiences were *not* sharply divided. Mayhew's costermonger liked melodrama *and* dancing and popular song: the division between drama and music hall, imposed by the licensing laws, did not reflect a division in taste.

What divided the audience along social class lines more than anything was the *behaviour* in music halls and theatres; the reputation of

LEFT: *Theatre was genuinely popular entertainment in the nineteenth century. A gathering (including a prostitute) outside the Victoria Theatre in the Cut, Lambeth (now the Old Vic).*

LEFT: *A programme for the Canterbury Music Hall. Although most people today think of music hall as being comic entertainment and popular songs, ballet and light opera often featured.*

places, the district of London they were in, and the stigma attached to drinking. This was brought out in an exchange between a member of the Select Committee of 1866 and John Buckstone, manager of the Haymarket Theatre:

> *Q: Provided that people did not eat and drink to excess and that they conducted themselves with propriety, what objection is there to a man sitting at a table taking his refreshments, and at the same time being amused by the performance on stage?*
> *A (BUCKSTONE): He cannot pay proper attention to the performance while he is eating.*
> *Q: What do you call proper attention?*
> *A: A man with his mouth full cannot pay proper attention to the performance.*
> *Q: He does not eat with his ears.*
> *A: But eating must interfere with listening.*
> *Q: Suppose his mouth is full, and his ears open, does not he please himself by employing two of his senses instead of one?*
> *A: Some minds may find enjoyment that way; but I think it is very sensual.*

This Commons Committee recommended an end to the division between music hall and theatre, but nothing was done for nearly fifty years. Although music halls introduced more and more dramatic sketches, and skirmished with the theatres, the music hall–theatrical division remained. So these two forms of popular entertainment were confined to different theatres. Melodrama and music hall were both in great demand, and were in counter-point to each other: love and murder in one, the lighter side of life in the other.

Love and murder

Love and murder – the essential ingredients of melodrama – pulled in the crowds all over London, from the lowly Bower Saloon in Lambeth, which specialized in 'dog dramas' in which canine heroes like the Newfoundland, Carlo, rescued people nightly, to Drury Lane which, towards the end of the nineteenth century, became the home of spectacular productions.

The galleries of theatres like the Victoria (now the Old Vic) were packed with youngsters aged between nine and twenty-three who whistled, shouted and sang their way through an evening's entertainment which would include a number of melodramatic plays, with

swooning heroines, scheming villains, noble heroes and stock comics. In between the dramas, which were acted in short scenes often ending with a 'tableau', would be singing and dancing. On one night when Mayhew visited the gallery of the Victoria, there was a crowd of between 1,500 and 2,000 youths, both boys and girls, responding vigorously to a melodrama, calling out to the actors, laughing at some scenes and greatly applauding a sailor dancing a hornpipe. All the paraphernalia of the stage was familiar to these theatre-goers, who were intolerant of any delays:

... should the interval appear too long, someone will shout out – referring to the curtain – 'Pull up that there winder blind! Or they

will call to the orchestra, saying, 'Now then you cat-gut scrapers, let's have a ha'purth of liveliness.' Neither will they allow a play to proceed until they have a good view of the stage, and 'higher the blue' is constantly shouted, when the sky is too low, or 'Light up the moon' when the transparency is rather dim.

There was the nautical melodrama, the Gothic melodrama, the animal melodrama: all the themes that were essentially universal. Whatever their setting they had a stock cast of characters which Michael Booth, in his classic study *English Melodrama*, identifies as hero, villain, heroine, old man, old woman, comic man, comic woman. Typically, the hero is very strong and trustworthy, but not very clever, and spends most of the play in deep trouble, issuing sermons against evil, while the villain schemes and drives the plot along, duping the hero, until fate intervenes to ensure the triumph of good over evil.

An essential ingredient of melodrama, enhancing any mood from the tragic to the comic – for they all had comic interludes – was the music. The orchestra did not necessarily play continuously, but struck up doleful chords as the heroine swooned in death, or provided tension and a sense of expectation, just as incidental music does in films. There was also an elaborate set of stage sound effects, from the thunder machines which a number of London theatres still have (lead balls rolled down a wood trough nailed zigzag to the back wall of the stage) to wind machines, and boxes of beans for the rain. Gas lighting and the use of limelight – a stick of quicklime heated with gas jets and producing a powerful beam concentrated by a lens – gave the spectacle a brilliance and eerie magic.

Of all the stock characters in melodrama, it is perhaps the villain who, throughout the period of its greatest popularity, is the key. Whatever his background, poor or wealthy, he elicited from the audience both hatred and admiration. He was the embodiment of evil, and his eventual defeat was the triumph of good. Along the way, however, in his raucous exchanges with the theatre gallery, he touched nerves and exposed them; though they wanted good to triumph, evil had its fascination. And he survives today in the horror movie, the film cartoon and much popular film drama, as Michael Booth says 'both repellent and attractive, frightening and magnetising'.

Since melodrama as a form of theatre dates from the late eighteenth century, it is tempting to regard it as a staged conflict of the tensions of the great metropolis itself, which promised both a better life to

LEFT: *A cut-out figure for a toy theatre – this one is plain and would have cost a penny, the coloured figures costing twopence. All the characters were taken from real theatrical productions, and showed well-known actors. The popularity of the toy theatre corresponded with a decline in actual theatre-going by respectable people.*

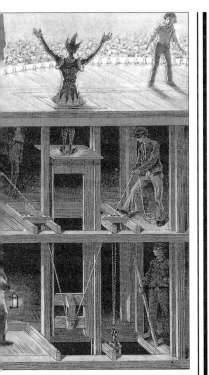

ABOVE: *All kinds of sensational effects were employed in popular Victorian theatre. This illustration shows the 'star trap' in which characters appeared miraculously on stage, fired through a segmented opening and usually in a puff of smoke. A trap like this is currently in use at the New London Theatre in the production* Cats.

those who moved to London from rural areas, and ruination and the loss of bucolic bliss. In popular plays there is, in fact, a very strong vein of the country lad or lass falling on hard times in the big city. Many of these melodramas, with titles such as *The Streets of London* (1864), *Lost in London* (1867) or *The Lights o'London* (1881), were given realistic and familiar settings on stage. In origin, however, they might be adaptations from French or American plays. Dion Boucicault, who wrote a great many, was an Irishman who lived for some time in America, and took many plays from the French. The emotions given voice in the melodrama were universal, even if the immediate setting was London.

Penny plain, twopence coloured

Melodrama appealed to the middle classes as much as to the poorer classes in London, certainly until about the 1870s or 1880s. However, it is generally accepted in histories of the theatre that from the early 1800s until the 1870s a significant number of the more respectable classes stayed away from the theatres. This was not so much because of the kind of performance they put on – although that may have been a factor – but because of the nature of the theatres themselves. The area around Drury Lane and Covent Graden in the mid-nineteenth century had become very run-down, and the streets teemed with the ragged poor, with prostitutes and thieves. Until a new kind of drama and a new kind of theatre was created by the efforts of actor-managers from the 1840s onwards (see Chapter Four), drama written specifically for the middle classes was at a low ebb. Charles Dickens loved the theatre and acted in amateur productions himself, but he wrote little for it. There was much more money to be made from novels, which could be appreciated in the home by those classes whose domestic comforts were greatly improved. It was in this context that one of the most charming – and in some ways the most puzzling – episodes in the history of nineteenth-century drama was acted out. This was the vogue for 'toy theatres' or what was known as the 'juvenile drama'. What the toy theatre productions have preserved wonderfully in miniature form is popular taste in theatre in the first half of the nineteenth century. They include, amongst many others, some of the great pantomime productions, as well as the 'hippodrama' *The Battle of Waterloo* which was staged at Astley's Amphitheatre, the home of circus and horsemanship.

The origins of the toy theatre are obscure, but it is well established

that they first became popular around 1812 when a number of printers began to produce sheets of characters for stage plays, sold as a 'penny plain, twopence coloured'. Often the names of the actors in the original stage production were given. These small figures were cut out, placed on the end of the little rods and a production could be put on with full scene changes in a beautifully designed theatre. Quite often they burned down, just as real theatres did, for they were supplied with footlights in which oil was burned. The text of the plays was usually carefully condensed to limit the time of the performance, and scores were available to accompany the action with melodramatic music. An orchestra pit was painted along the bottom of the stage, with musicians in full melody.

An enduring and favourite production was the melodrama *The Miller and his Men*, which was first performed at Covent Garden in 1813. In a review of the play, *The Morning Post* critic wrote:

... it is made up of the usual melo-dramatic ingredients viz thunder and lightning, bewildered travellers, hospitable cottagers, and jolly robbers ... to look for probability in a Melo-Drama would be almost as ridiculous as to see it in a Harlequinade; and to complain of the un-natural exclamations of its heroes no less unreasonable than it would be to denounce the blunders of the Clown as things which cannot be and therefore ought not to be pictured. The

LEFT: *A classic melodrama,* The Streets of London, *popular in the nineteenth century. It was, in fact, an adaptation of an American play,* The Poor of New York.

Eiber   *Karl.*

Miller and his Men are guilty of many extravagances; some of the incidents which occur are poor but an agreeable bustle is kept up from the beginning of the piece to its end. Several of the situations are good and the explosion of a mill at the conclusion treating the audience with a blow-up made it go off with boundless éclat. The scenery is particularly beautiful. The music by Mr Bishop is pleasing and appropriate; and the acting throughout is good.

This Covent Garden production was one of the first to be reproduced for the toy theatre and was put on sale by William West in 1813. It remained a popular melodrama and was the favourite production for toy theatres, with versions produced by Webb and Pollock and many other printers and illustrators until about the 1860s.

The cost of the theatres and a full production was such that it must have been the middle classes who were buying them. There is a school of thought which says that in their earliest years they were bought by adults, as domestic versions of popular plays, rather like a quaint version of the modern video. But for the most part, they appear to have appealed to children – hence the term 'juvenile drama' – and especially to boys.

There is a nice anecdote about Charles Dickens's love of toy theatre when he was a schoolboy at Wellington House Academy in the Hampstead Road. A fellow pupil, Dr Henry Danson, recalled much later how much Dickens had enjoyed toy theatricals:

We mounted small theatres and got up very gorgeous scenery to illustrate 'The Miller and his Men' and 'Cherry and Fair Star'. I remember the present Mr Beverly, the scene painter, assisted us in this. Dickens was always the leader in these plays, which were occasionally presented with much solemnity before an audience of boys in the presence of the ushers.

My brother, assisted by Dickens, got up 'The Miller and his Men' in a very gorgeous form. Master Beverly constructed the mill for us in such a way that it could tumble to pieces with the assistance of crackers. At one representation the fireworks in the last scene ending with the destruction of the mill were so very real that the police interfered and knocked violently at the doors.

To what extent families enjoyed these productions in the dark and cluttered Victorian home before the mid-century we really do not know, although there are illustrations which suggest that they were

Miller

Lothair

put on with piano accompaniment and appreciated by a family audience. But by the 1860s they had become more and more a boy's toy, and some were given away with boys' magazines. They still had their enthusiasts late in the century, among them the young Winston Churchill. By this time, their heyday was over, though two of the most prolific producers, Webb and Pollock, were still selling toy theatres in the 1930s.

Writing in 1932, A.E. Wilson provides the most generally accepted account of the rise and fall of the toy theatre, and the way in which its fortunes reflected theatrical taste among those who bought them. In *Penny Plain, Twopence Coloured*, he says:

> *Primarily the decline of the vogue is bound up with the advance of the English stage. Its vogue or entire history as a living thing, and not as a subject of interest only to the collector or antiquary, may be taken to extend roughly from the beginning of the century to the 1870s. The drama had ceased to be a drama of violence and action, and of crude emotion; it was becoming the drama of plain realism ... Here to my mind you have one of the most damaging of the many blows dealt at the Juvenile Drama; it was being deprived of the very substance upon which it had thrived ... exciting combats, violent encounters, sanguinary duels, the display of guns, pistols, swords, and other deadly engines, and every form of violent action.*

In addition to this mortal blow to the toy theatre, the decline in middle-class taste for old-style melodrama, there was the rise of illustrated boys' magazines, the coming of photography with its exact representation of scenes, and finally the moving picture.

Melodrama comes to the silver screen

Melodrama on stage did not disappear with the demise of the toy theatre, however. It remained immensely popular in the theatres of Lambeth, the East End and the working-class districts of London until the early 1900s. And in the West End it continued to draw the crowds to Drury Lane, the Adelphi and the Princess's. It was the refined, middle-class London audience that turned to what was called 'tea cup and saucer' theatre, the comedy set in the drawing room, without blood and thunder or dramatic stage effects. But this was only a small section of the audience. From the mid-nineteenth century (see Chapter Five) the West End was drawing in a provincial audience who could get up to town and return home in a day on the railways. This wider audience was still enthralled by such lavish productions as *The Whip*

ABOVE, LEFT AND RIGHT: *Cut-out scenes from the most popular production of the toy theatre, the melodrama* The Miller and His Men. *A favourite among boys was the explosion which ends the play: as a schoolboy, Dickens made such a noise with the blowing up of the mill that the police were called.*

at Drury Lane, which included a spectacular scene on stage in which a train was derailed.

From the early 1900s 'love and murder' enjoyed its greatest period of popularity for it was the perfect material for silent films, many of which in the early days were simply filmed versions of stage plays.

As in the theatre, the musical accompaniment to silent films – always live – was important. Stan Shevills recalls:

LEFT AND TOP RIGHT: Scenes from what became known as 'tea-cup and saucer' theatre, which became popular with the middle classes in the latter half of the nineteenth century.

The pianist at the Premiere Cinema never seemed to look at the keys of the piano. She just kept her eyes glued to the screen and played at a tempo that moved with the pace of the film as it went. And I can remember a film that I did see, Hunchback of Notre Dame; *it was a horrifying film as far as I was concerned. Lon Cheney was the actor. I remember my father saying he was a master of make-up and disguise and he had the most distorted features. He looked horrible with his hunchback as well, and when he was climbing up towards the pinnacles of the towers before he leapt out into space the pianist was just banging away, banging away getting louder and louder, and there was an enormous crash at the finish as he dived into space and everybody sort of gasped. It was the pianist that built it up.*

'Angela: Why did you ask me to pretend to love my fan?

From the country

A new technique was the serial, a melodrama in episodes with a cliff-hanger finish. Frank Simmonds saw these silent melodramas as a boy:

The serial was a continuing story but at the end of each day's episode, of course, somebody was in a situation, a perilous situation which you couldn't possibly see a way out of. This was the cliff-hanger end and at the point where you thought, 'This is it, they are going to die,' up would come a message on the screen. 'To be continued next week'. So of course you had to start all over again. But it was all a bit of a cheat really ... You got a situation where somebody was being tied down to a railway track and a train [was] rushing towards them, and it would finish up when they were about two yards away, no possible way of getting out of it. The following week it would start up when the train was a quarter of a mile down the track, you see, and somebody would be cutting the ropes – so by the time the train was two yards away, the man was walking away. This was the sort of thing that you got.

The fact that most of the films shown were American is not, as you might imagine, a significant change, for the origins of a great many of the most popular melodramas were French, or German, or indeed American. For example, one of the most popular melodramas of the 'cloak and sword' variety, which played not only in the East End but was a showpiece of the great Henry Irving at the Lyceum in the West End in the 1880s, was Dion Boucicault's *The Corsican Brothers*, which was in turn an adaptation of a French stage production of a novel by Alexander Dumas. Another of Boucicault's plays, *The Streets of London*, was taken from an American play called *The Poor of New York*. A great deal of popular British entertainment in the nineteenth century had its origins in America and there was continuous traffic both ways across the Atlantic of both stage actors and actresses and music hall stars.

RIGHT: *A scene from one of the most popular plays of nineteenth-century theatre,* The Corsican Brothers, *adapted from the French by Dion Boucicault. It involved many special effects, and the invention of the Corsican trap in which the ghost of one brother emerges slowly from below stage.*

ABOVE: *In the Thirties, Hollywood films were much more popular with London audiences than British films which were regarded as 'unreal' and narrowly middle class.*

The fact that the Americans were better at cine-melodrama than British film-makers was, it could be argued, because of the way in which British theatre had developed to satisfy the tastes of a middle-class audience. By the 1930s, American movies struck London audiences as being much more real and relevant to their lives than the home-spun dramas. In a survey of East End tastes for *World Film News* in 1937, Richard Carr reported on 'People's Pictures and People's Palaces'. One cinema manager summed it up:

East End audiences are very critical. They like good pictures, good American pictures, pictures of movement and action. They won't stand British pictures here at any price ... How do I know what they like and what they don't like? I have a job not to know. If the regular patrons don't like a film, they make a point of telling me afterwards. They say 'B... y awful film, that', or some such remark. Or else they clap their hands during the film, or shuffle their feet and whistle. They certainly let me know whether or not they like the films we show.

A summary of a report by film exhibitors published by *World Film News* in 1937 had this to say on taste in working-class areas:

Again and again exhibitors of this category complain of 'old school tie' standards inherent in so many British Films. They describe the 'horse laughs' with which the Oxford accents of supposed crooks are greeted and the impatience of their patrons with the well-worked social drama type of filmed stageshow. Similarly the lack of action and the excess of superfluous dialogue are censured ... Films with tempo and action, stirring in their appeal, simple and straight-forward in treatment and related to the lives of the people, appear to be the type preferred in this group. Comedy and slapstick are also required. Romance and melodrama of the better type are popular.

Among middle-class audiences, British films were favoured.

The lighter side of life

By the 1930s, when the old melodrama theatres had been turned into cinemas, that other great Victorian creation in popular taste, music hall, still survived, although with nothing like its old vigour or style. From its beginnings in the mid-nineteenth century, it had flourished in the 1890s and had become easily the most popular form of enter-tainment. The music hall stars were the greatest stars, and they had

ABOVE: *The first super-star of music hall, George Leybourne, who invented the character* Champagne Charlie, *a city swell who lived the good life. Leybourne appealed largely to an audience of young men: he died at the age of 42, having lived the life he sang about.*

the highest pay and the largest following. Once they were famous they were cheered on stage before they spoke a word and often the audience would begin to sing their signature tune.

Such was the reputation of music hall in its heyday, and so strongly has it been presented as *the* expression of popular taste in the Victorian and Edwardian period, that this distorted view is hard to re-focus. It is regarded as quintessentially British, and specifically very London and very cockney. It is quite true that much of it was. But music hall was never simply a straightforward vulgar comment on working-class life, and many aspects of it are extremely difficult to interpret.

In its early days – the 1860s and 1870s – the music hall had a very young audience, and the first of its superstars, George Leybourne, made his name as a flashily dressed swell. He was famous as *Champagne Charlie*, 'good at any time of day or night, boys, for a spree'. Just as pop singers set fashion so did Leybourne. The appeal of stars such as Leybourne was obviously to an audience finding its feet in the big city, wanting to have a good time, to explore the night spots, but also through their common enjoyment to feel a sense of belonging to the knowing crowd of the metropolis. It was later that musical hall appealed to a more mature, married audience, reflecting many of the concerns of everyday life.

It is very difficult for a modern audience to understand the meaning of many of the best-known songs for a Victorian London audience. To take just one example, there is Marie Lloyd's famous rendition of *My Old Man says 'Follow the Van'*. To those who packed the great halls of the late nineteenth century, the words made a very specific reference to an experience many Londoners in poorer districts had had doing a 'moonlight flit' to avoid the rent man:

> We had to move away,
> 'Cos the rent we couldn't pay,
> The moving van came round just after dark;
> There was me and my old man,
> Shoving things inside the van,
> Which we'd often done before, let me remark . . .

It then goes into the celebrated chorus of 'My old man said "Follow the Van, and Don't Dilly Dally on the way!" Off went the cart with the home packed in it, I walked behind with my old cock linnet . . .'

Although the surviving recordings of Marie Lloyd are sadly very poor, the sweetness of her voice and of the music accompanying these

BELOW: *In the first great music hall boom, one of the favourite characters was the flashily dressed man-about-town, with enormous whiskers known as 'Piccadilly weepers'. Like later pop stars, they set fashion and style.*

ABOVE: *One of the greatest of music hall stars, Gus Elen, who was at his height of fame in the 1890s. He is pictured here in 1932 when he recorded three of his hit songs for the film company, Pathé.*

gritty songs is striking. Rumbustious revivals of the old favourites completely miss the subtlety of these songs and the use of gesture by the singers to mime the action. Very few of the old singers survived into the age of talking films: Marie Lloyd died in 1922. But there is one great artist who was big in the 1890s and who made a come-back in 1932 to record three numbers for Pathé. Though the recordings were shot in a studio without an audience to roar the chorus – an essential element in all music-hall songs – they are the nearest anyone can get today to the sound of the late Victorian period. The performer is a Londoner, Gus Elen, and the three numbers are 'It's a Great Big Shame', 'The Postman's Holiday' and 'Half a Pint of Ale'.

The first of these begins:

> I've lost a pal, 'e's the best in all the tahn
> But don't you fink 'im dead, because 'e ain't –
> But since 'e's wed 'e 'as 'ad ter knuckle dahn –
> It's enuf to wex the temper of a saint!
>
> 'E's a brewer's drayman wiv a leg o'mutton fist,
> An' as strong as a bullick or an 'orse –
> Yet in 'er 'ands 'e's like a little kid –
> Oh! I wish I could get 'im a divorce.
>
> CHORUS
> It's a great big shame, an' if she belonged ter me
> I'd let 'er know who's who –
> [here Elen shapes up with an open hand to threaten the wife]
> Naggin' at a feller wot is six foot three
> And 'er only four foot two!
> Oh! they 'adn't been married not a month nor more,
> When underneath her fumb goes Jim –
> Oh isn't it a pity that the likes of 'er
> Should put upon the likes of 'im!

The song is surprisingly melodic, and delivered in mime with a kind of intense ferocity, as if Gus Elen really is upset about the loss of his mate to marriage. It is full of little comments, such as the illustration of his pal's strength with the reference to the fact that it takes two policemen to arrest him and another six to hold him down.

Writing in the abstract about music-hall songs is hopeless, for it gives no feel at all for the vigour of the performance or the meaning.

THE F[...]

Sung with the Greatest Success By

MISS·VES[...]

Copyright.   LONDON: FRANCIS, DAY & H[...]
Publishers of Smallwood's Celebrated Pianoforte Tut[...]
NEW YORK, T.B.HARMS[...]
Copyright MDCCCXX in the United S[...]

ABOVE AND RIGHT: *Vesta Tilley, one of the great male impersonators of the Victorian music hall, who sang such songs as 'Good Luck to the Girl who loves a Sailor', was a London star from 1878 until her farewell performance at the Coliseum in 1920.*

There were many songs about men and women, about marriage, about people who got above their station and acted like toffs, about people down on their uppers trying to maintain their dignity, about naughtiness at the seaside, about getting drunk. Men made fun of women, and women made fun of men. There was very little reflection of some of the harshest realities of the day, of death and disease. But then music hall was resolutely against serious comment about anything: for that there was melodrama, although there were lots of political nationalist music hall songs around 1870 and again at the time of the Boer War.

This suggests one important clue to the appeal of much music hall: it was a place you could feel at home, familiar with life in the big city. The songs were full of little references and innuendo which you could understand. Just as melodrama was interspersed with comic episodes, so sentimental songs in music hall would be broken by some patter from the singer. Harry Lauder would break off from singing 'Roamin' in the Gloamin' to amuse the audience with a story about how he was engaged but had lost the engagement ring. Then he would give a rendition of 'Keep Right on to the End of the Road'.

Writing in 1948 in *Twenty Shillings in the Pound*, the colourful, prolific and infuriatingly imprecise writer on London entertainment, W. MacQueen-Pope, had this to say of music hall:

> *The music hall ... was a club of the clubless. It gave the people what they wanted in the manner in which they wanted it, in a way they understood. It sang and it pattered of the unpaid rent, the mother-in-law, the lodger, kippers, erring wives and husbands. It joked about physical violence, seaside holidays and beer. It jeered at foreigners, it glorified this country. It gave the people their patriotism in doses hot and strong.*

This might be a fair description of much of music hall in its heyday between the 1880s and around 1910, but it omits some of the most intriguing elements in popular taste, perhaps the kind of thing Lenin had in mind when, in 1907, he wrote to Gorky:

> *In the London music halls there is a certain satirical or sceptical attitude towards the common-place, there is an attempt to turn it inside-out, to distrust it somewhat, to point up the illogicality of the everyday. Abstruse – but interesting.*

The costermonger interviewed in the 1850s by Mayhew referred to 'nigger music', which he says has gone out of fashion. It may have

ABOVE: *Dan Leno, one of the most celebrated music hall comedians, began on the stage at the age of four, at one time played a 'nigger minstrel' and became best known as a pantomime dame in Drury Lane pantomime. He died at the age of forty-three.*

done so briefly, in that area at that time, but this extraordinary form of popular entertainment in fact endured in one form or another from the 1830s until it became socially unacceptable in the 1970s. Its last manifestation was *The Black and White Minstrel Show* on television in the 1960s.

Its history begins, in fact, before music hall proper got going. In 1836 a white American performer called T.D. Rice arrived in London and caused a sensation at the Surrey and Adelphi theatres with his performance of a song and dance routine called Jim Crow. For his stage act, Rice blacked his face with burned cork, and sang with a kind of plantation patois, a simple little song like an Americanized jig tune, while he danced a strange, soft-shoe shuffle. He was dressed as a ragged black from the Deep South. He was the first 'nigger minstrel' to appear in London and began a craze which soon produced many imitators among English performers, and drew many more blacked-up whites across the Atlantic.

Today it is impossible to find any clue as to the cause of Rice's success in the words of the original song:

> *I come from Old Kentucky. A long time ago*
> *Where I first larn to wheel about*
> *And jump Jim Crow*
> *Wheel about, and turn about, and do jis so,*
> *Ebry time I wheel about I jump Jim Crow.*

The American historian Robert C. Toll in his study *Blacking Up*, argues that the genre appealed to northern white Americans who were intrigued to know what slaves were actually like. He also says that the dance was critical for the success of these first performers, and the start of a long period in which Afro-American dances swept the world. But their meaning for London audiences must have been quite different. It may be significant that the popularity followed closely on the abolition of slavery in 1833: perhaps there was an unconscious celebration of what the British regarded as their liberality, after years of making a fortune out of the slave trade.

It is notoriously difficult to make sense of these popular fads, and it is virtually impossible to theorize about them without appearing to be pretentious. What it is possible to say is that the 'nigger minstrel' represented in London from the 1830s until the end of the century a kind of popular entertainment that appealed to a very wide section of the population. The terms 'nigger' and 'coon' were used quite freely and though they were clearly patronizing they did not carry the modern racist meaning. Although there had been a vogue for keeping black servants, and black people were sometimes seen in the dockland areas, they were unfamiliar figures to most Londoners.

The minstrel performers were not, of course, black, but white performers playing the part of a simple, lovable, comical, romantic caricature of a black, a freed slave from the mythical land of Dixie. The make-up was a disguise, and the character unplaceable in London society, which is no doubt the reason their performances were so widely acceptable, without the social stigma that was attached by the middle classes to much music hall entertainment. In *Minstrel Memories*, published in 1928, Harry Reynolds says:

> *Straightlaced people who even barred the ordinary theatre patronised St James's Hall. It was quite an ordinary experience to observe a dozen clergymen at one time enjoying the minstrels' entertainment; so naturally their flocks followed.*

At first there appears to have been some confusion in the minds of Londoners who were thrilled by the performances of the minstrels. It was a popular gimmick amongst showmen to exhibit all kinds of exotic specimens of mankind in their booths: wild and interesting Zulu, for example. The first fully fledged minstrel troupe to arrive in England, Dan Emmett's Virginia Minstrels who appeared at the Adelphi Theatre in 1843, billed themselves as 'the only representatives of the Negro that have appeared in this country'. They were all white, as were the Ethiopian Serenaders who toured in 1846 and who were accused sometimes of being fake blacks, which they were.

Much of the appeal of the minstrels appears to have been in the combination of a catchy tune, an intriguing dance, and words which were very easily adapted to topical subjects. In the Jim Crow song books there is, for example, Jim Crow's visit to the Lord Mayor's Show:

> *Good people give attention*
> *And listen to Jim Crow*
> *While him sing a little ditty*
> *Called de Lord Mayor's show*
>
> *Push along, shove along*
> *Jim Crow without delay*
> *Will sing de fun and frolic*
> *Of de Lord Mayor's Day*

ABOVE: *The song cover for the original 'nigger minstrel' sensation, Jim Crow, sung and danced by the American T.D. Rice. Rice arrived in London from America in 1836 and began a craze which lasted in various forms until the Black and White Minstrels of television.*

I started from de 'Delphe
To the City I declare
And when I got to Cheapside
O dear, what sights were dere

Den run along, shove along
And do jist so
Or dey will roll you in the gutter
At de Lord Mayor's show.

There were hundreds of songs like this. Whether the performers made much of the 'plantation-speak' we do not know, but the records of later minstrels such as Eugene Stratton, popular at the end of the century, suggest that the performers were quite anglicized.

Minstrel troupes became popular from the 1840s and developed their own complete stage acts, which were a mixture of song, dance and banal humour, with the 'stump' speech a speciality. Recognizable characters emerged, sitting at either end of the line of minstrels, usually called Banjo and Bones, the latter providing rhythmic background. In time these minstrel troupes set up in their own halls, the Christy Minstrels playing at St James's Hall in Piccadilly, and the Mohawk Minstrels at the Agricultural Hall in Islington. It was said that the audiences of the Mohawks were chiefly country folk come to London for the Agricultural show, whereas the St James's Hall audience was rather refined. The Mohawks evolved a London style of minstrelsy and their shows from the 1870s until the end of the century included orchestras and choirs which on 'specials' nights would sing Irish, Scottish, or 'Plantation' songs.

Minstrel performances were ideal for street entertainers who copied the acts in the halls. Easily the best account of what these shows were like around 1860 is given in Henry Mayhew's interviews with street minstrels in the 1850s. One man from a 'school' of nigger minstrels described the clothing:

> *We are regularly full-dressed, in fashionable black coats and trousers, open white waistcoats, pumps... and wigs to imitate the real negro head of hair ... each man made his own wig out of horse-hair dyed black, and sewn with black thread on to the skin of an old silk hat.*

The most popular numbers, he said, were 'Old Mr Coon', 'Buffalo Gals', 'Going Ober de Mountain', and others in the same vein, including the

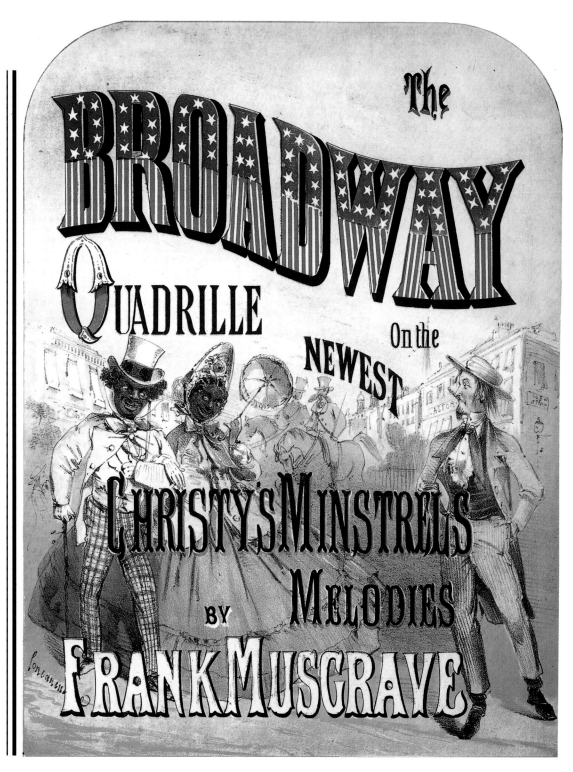

ABOVE: *G.H. Elliott, one of the most popular of the 'burned cork' minstrel artists, who called himself 'The Chocolate Coloured Coon' and sang such songs as 'Lily of Laguna', and 'If the Man in the Moon were a Coon'.*

still remembered 'Oh Susannah', a typical nonsense song with lines like 'the sun so hot I froze myself'.

Another minstrel recounted to Mayhew some of the patter the troupe would offer between songs:

Perhaps we'd do another conundrum, such as this: 'Supposing you nigger was dead, what would be the best time to bury you?' One says, 'I shan't suppose'. Another says, 'I don't know'. And then I say, 'Why, the latter end of the summer' and one asks, 'Why Jim?' 'Because it's the best time for black berrying'. Then I cry out, 'Now you niggers, go on with the consort' and one of them will add, 'Now, Jim, we'll have that lemonoholy song of Dinah Clare, that poor girl that fell in the water-butt and got burn to death.'

This kind of nonsense was out of fashion by the end of the century, but the minstrel was popular in music hall and lighter forms of theatre in the Victorian era and remained a feature of variety in the Twenties and Thirties. Indeed the first talking film, *The Jazz Singer*, includes Al Jolson blacked up as a minstrel. By this time, most of the songs were sentimental, notably 'Lily of Laguna', or 'Sue, Sue Sue' as sung by G.H. Elliott. The minstrel show, like all other kinds of entertainment, evolved continuously and was absorbed into other things, particularly the soft-shoe style of dancing, of which Elliott was a master.

Hippodrama, or heroic horses

The minstrel entertainers had first become popular in London in that period when the theatre was in disarray. Legitimate drama was still, technically, the preserve of the Patent Theatres, Covent Garden and Drury Lane. But many minor theatres had been built, and had what was known as a 'burletta' licence: they could put on musicals, in effect defined in a vague and unsatisfactory way by the custom and practice of the Lord Chamberlain's Office. However, the Patent Houses had difficulty drawing an audience with straight drama, and from early in the nineteenth century abandoned any pretence that they were upholding the national drama.

When the managers cast around for a form of entertainment that would fill their vast theatres after they had been re-built (Covent Garden 1809, Drury Lane 1812), they were much impressed by a novel form of theatre that had been founded in the late eighteenth century. This was hippodrama, in which some of the principal actors and stars were trained horses.

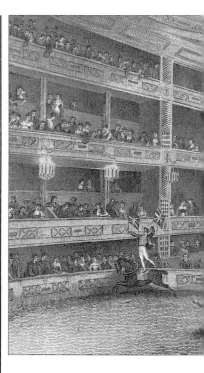

ABOVE AND RIGHT: *The home of horse play, or hippodrama, Astley's Amphitheatre, which was founded just south of Westminster Bridge and was popular until the second half of the nineteenth century.*

Performing animals of various kinds had been providing amusement for Londoners for a long time, of course, and continued to do so in stage productions, as they do now on film. But equestrian drama was a genuine innovation, and became popular not only in London, but in Paris and New York. The originator was a retired sergeant major from General Elliott's Light Dragoons, Philip Astley. He began with exhibitions of trick horse-riding in an open field in 1768. As his performances grew in popularity, with the inclusion of acrobats and the kind of variety that could be found at Bartholomew Fair, he began to roof in the site. Astley's became a proper circus in 1779 – some would say the first ever circus in the world. In 1782, a rival to Astley's opened as the Royal Circus and Philharmonic Academy, just down the road; this was to become later the Surrey Theatre. The Royal Circus had, as well as the sawdust ring, a stage on which various kinds of concerts and drama might be performed. Astley's copied this innovation, and the stage was set for the development of hippodrama. The special attraction of a visit to Astley's is captured in this description from Charles Dickens's *Old Curiosity Shop*:

> *Dear, dear, what a place it looked that Astley's; with all the paint, gilding and looking-glass; the vague smell of horses suggestive of coming wonders; the curtain that hid such gorgeous mysteries; the clear white sawdust in the circus; the company coming in and taking their places; the fiddlers looking carelessly up at them while they tuned their instruments. What feverish excitement when the little bell rang and the music began in good earnest, with strong parts for the drum, and sweet effects for the triangles! Well might Barbara's mother say to Kit's mother that the gallery was the place to see from, and wonder that it wasn't much dearer than the boxes.*
>
> *... Little Jacob applauded till his hands were sore; Kit cried 'ankor' at the end of everything; and Barbara's mother beat her umbrella on the floor, in her ecstasies, until it was nearly worn down to the gingham.*

Not all of what was put on at Astley's was, strictly speaking, hippodrama, but the kind of horsemanship that can still be see at the circus: men and women jumping on and off galloping steeds, or riding two or more at once. But in much of what was done a plot was introduced, and hippodramas were actually written with key parts for the horses which were trained to drop dead and remain dead on stage, to rise and descend through stage traps, to behave wildly and to gallop

ABOVE: *One of the most celebrated 'hippodramas' at Astley's was* Mazeppa, *in which a young man (played in this case by one of the star horse trainers and riders, Andrew Ducrow) was strapped to a wild horse which galloped off stage, up a ramp, at great risk to itself and the rider.*

off-stage on ramps, to fetch things with their teeth and to sit with a bib on and eat a meal.

Perhaps the greatest exponent of hippodrama, and certainly the finest horseman of his day, was Andrew Ducrow. Ducrow was born in 1793 into a circus family and, like many performers of the day, first performed on stage at a young age. He played in pantomime at Drury Lane in 1814, and he was a famous horseman in the 1820s. In 1825, he took over the management of Astley's where he thrilled audiences with his dare-devil riding as *The Wild Indian Hunter*. Ducrow invented, too, his Grecian poses on horseback, imitating famous statues in the flesh.

At first, the Royal Circus and Astleys used their circus rings for displays of horsemanship and their stages for drama as two separate forms of entertainment. But from 1800 they began to combine the two and hippodrama was born. Philip Astley's son, John, achieved one of his first great successes in 1807 with *The Brave Cossack: or Perfidy Punished*, a melodrama on horseback. According to *The Times* review of 8 May 1807, 'the noble effect of a troop of horse in full speed, in the very act of attack and defence, drew such reiterated plaudits, as must be seen to be believed'.

As hippodrama developed, all the latest stage effects were used to heighten the excitement. As A.H. Saxon points out in his definitive history of this kind of entertainment, *Enter Foot and Horse*, the fatality rate of both horses and riders was considerable over the years, as they plunged through traps, or slipped on ramps. But this did not prevent the stampede of equestrian drama, which soon spread from Astley's to the Patent Theatres. Drury Lane had had horses on its stage in the late eighteenth century. The production of *Blue Beard or Female Curiosity* at Covent Garden in 1811, then managed by John Philip Kemble, was a hippodrama. It had two great scenes employing trained horses, and was followed by *Timour the Tartar*. Crowds flocked to the spectacle and Covent Garden's receipts rose impressively. Horses and riders from Astley's were regularly employed. At the same time Astley's own productions

RIGHT: *The menagerie of the astonishing tamer of wild beasts, the American Isaac Van Amburgh, whose performances in pantomime and opera at Drury Lane thrilled the young Queen Victoria – in particular when he snatched the lamb from the leopard's mouth. This painting is by Landseer.*

became more and more lavish, encompassing entire cavalry charges as in the production of *The Battle of Waterloo*, first performed in 1824 and seen by the Duke of Wellington himself. The ultimate in hippodrama came in the 1856–7 season, when the then manager of Astley's, William Cooke, hit upon the idea of Shakespeare on horseback. The first and most successful of these productions was *Richard III*, in which the highlight was the Battle of Bosworth Field, with the King's horse lying 'dead' in the final scene while the battle crashed all around it.

From what evidence there is, it appears that hippodrama in its heyday from the early 1800s until the 1860s drew its audience from a wide section of the population, though serious drama critics for the most part dismissed it, and were especially outraged by its appearance at Covent Garden. Queen Victoria certainly was very fond of the circus, and as a girl in 1833 made sketches of Ducrow's performance at Astley's in *St George and the Dragon*.

In fact, the young Queen was enthralled by a number of productions with performing animals. Her greatest excitement was to see the American tamer of wild beasts, Isaac Van Amburgh, in the Christmas pantomime at Drury Lane in 1838–9, *Harlequin and Jack Frost*. In the eleventh scene, Van Amburgh ('He is a very strong man and has an awful squint of the eyes', Queen Victoria noted) appeared on stage with his menagerie of lions, lionesses, tigers, cheetahs and leopards. 'They all seem actuated by the most awful fear of him,' she wrote in her diary, '. . . he takes them by their paws, throws them down, makes them roar, and lies upon them after enraging them. It's quite beautiful to see, and makes me wish I could do the same!'

George Rowell in *Queen Victoria Goes to the Theatre* calculates that in 1839 the newly crowned monarch went to Drury Lane seven times in six weeks especially to see Van Amburgh, and was rewarded with an incident she described with wonder when things seemed to go wrong and a lamb placed before the lion was snatched by the leopard:

> . . . *all the others [animals] except the lion, and all those in the other cage making a rush to help in the slaughter; it was an awful moment and we thought all was over, when Van Amburgh rushed to the Leopard, tore the lamb unhurt from the Leopard, which he beat severely – took the lamb in his arms – only looked at the others, and not one moved, though in the act of devouring the lamb. It was beautiful and wonderful.*

As with so much in Victorian theatre, there was a street version of such stage performances. Henry Mayhew describes the itinerant exhibitors of 'Happy Families', cages filled with a collection of animals which by rights should have torn each other to shreds, but appeared to co-exist in peace. This account was given by a Happy Family exhibitor who showed at Waterloo Bridge and outside the National Gallery where, he said; the 'middle class of society' were his best supporters.

> *Hundreds have tried their hands at happy families, and have failed. The cat has killed the mice, and hawks have killed the birds, the dogs the rats, and even the cats the rats, the birds and even one another; indeed it has been anything but a happy family. By our system we never have a mishap; and have had animals eight or*

ABOVE: *This is a French illustration of a mechanism, used in London, to allow horses to gallop on stage while remaining in the same position. Drury Lane staged the Derby in this way in 1896, and many theatres had horse racing at one time or another. The newly opened Coliseum ran the Derby in 1904 on its enormous revolving stage.*

nine years in the cage – until they've died of age, indeed. In our present cage we have 58 birds and animals, and of 17 different kinds; 3 cats, 2 dogs (a terrier and a spaniel), 2 monkeys, 2 magpies, 2 jackdaws, 2 jays, 10 starlings (some of them talk), 6 pigeons, 2 hawks, 2 barn fowls, 1 screech owl, 5 common-sewer rats, 5 white rats (a novelty), 8 guinea pigs, 2 rabbits (1 wild and 1 tame), 1 hedgehog, and 1 tortoise.

This fascination with trained animals has been an enduring feature of London entertainment. In live entertainment it still survives, of course, in the circus, though without any of the thrill it once held for audiences. As with melodrama, a great deal of its theatrical appeal was stolen by film and ultimately by television. For example, the Derby was first filmed in 1896, at a time when Drury Lane was putting on a stage version with the horses running against a mechanically powered roller platform. In 1904, the Coliseum was running the Derby on its revolving stage, and was still competing with cinematic thrills in 1929 when it put on terrier racing. The dogs chased an electric rat.

Animal acts were popular in variety theatres well into this century: Lockhard's elephants, performing seals and poodles, lion taming and so on. But the last building dedicated to animal performance was the Hippodrome built in 1900 as a music hall and circus, with a huge water-tank for aquadrama – another popular theatrical form of the nineteenth century. The climax to the show was 29 elephants coming down a slide, and plunging in succession into the water tank! The Hippodrome has become purely a theatre of varieties before the First World War, then the home of musicals and in 1958 a cabaret *Talk of the Town*. It is now a discotheque.

Animals shows, and sometimes full-scale circuses, were included from time to time in the variety programmes of super-cinemas in the 1930s. John Huntley recalls one near-disastrous episode:

At the Gaumont, Hammersmith in 1938 we had our regular cine variety show but this year it was different – it was a circus. And one of the great things this time was that there were going to be elephants. And so we saw the feature film and then we saw the variety and then we had the second feature film. But this time the second feature film went on immediately after the first and we were puzzled. It turned out that they were all set to do the circus and they got the elephants into a lift and it had jammed. It took about 45 minutes to free them, and during that time of course these two elephants got very, very agitated indeed. Up went the lights and the elephants came on and one of them decided that he's had enough of it and made a run for it. And he lumbered across the stage with great dignity, charged into the orchestra, all the instruments went flying, and the whole of the orchestra disappeared out of the nearest available emergency exit. Leaving us – the audience – to confront this elephant which plodded solemnly towards us. The front row – of course it was packed, the cinema – leaped out of their seats and tried to climb over, I remember, to the second row. . . . fortunately it [the elephant] slowed up and it just began to meander up and down and then my last memory of it was a lady from the cafe, which used to be in the front of the cinema in those days, coming tearing down the aisles knocking everyone for six and saying, 'Get out of the way. Get out of the way'. She was armed with six enormous bags of buns and these were given to the elephant.

BELOW: *The London Hippodrome – literally a place for horse drama – opened in 1900, and staged many spectaculars with a vast water tank, including the production advertised here.*

THE TYPHOON

LONDON HIPPODROME TWICE DAILY AT 2 & 8.

A L'ALHAMBRA — A MOINS QUE CE NE SOIT A L'EMPIRE OU AU PALACE-THEATRE

RIGHT: *A common element in popular entertainment was, by the end of the nineteenth century, the chorus line of pretty girls: these are from the famous Alhambra music hall in Leicester Square, known for its massed troops of pretty dancers.*

Denis Norden as a young cinema manager also remembers the circus on stage at the Trocadero, Elephant & Castle.

Some of the cinemas had a very large area backstage, or they had a large car park, where they could stable the animals as it were. The trouble with the Elephant & Castle was it was very narrow backstage ... We couldn't get them in the car park so we put them behind the screen – all the animals including the lions, who were perfectly happy there. The only sign that they were there was that we had an MGM film that week and when the MGM lion came on at the beginning and roared, his mates behind the screen roared back!

Bring on the girls

Though the range of entertainment offered in Victorian London was enormously wide, the most popular forms nearly always had three elements present to stir the souls of an audience which craved relief from the tensions of metropolitan life. All popular entertainment, including hippodramas, had musical accompaniment. The trilling of the strings was vital to melodrama, the twanging of banjos and the click of 'bones' was integral to minstrelsy, every music-hall turn, except the solo comedian, had musical accompaniment. In all forms of popular entertainment, comic relief was offered between the dramatic episodes. And in nearly every form of entertainment, dancing of some kind or another was part of the show, whether it was the soft-shoe style, or clog dancing, or a hornpipe, or horses dancing as they did in hippodrama.

GAIETY THEATRE

MANAGING DIRECTOR   Mr. GEORGE EDWARDES

ABOVE: *The girls of the Gaiety Theatre were especially popular with a 'bohemian' – that is, not respectable – crowd, and some married wealthy men who had picked them out on stage.*

The stage play, in which there was no music and the audience sat silent expecting to be entertained simply by the power of the acting, without stage effects of any kind, was always a rarity. Even today, the most successful long-running productions shown to large audiences in London's West End involve stage effects, music, dance and song.

The musical, an American term, grew out of a fusion of a number of different forms of theatre and music hall. Its immediate forerunner was what was known as burlesque, the speciality of the Gaiety Theatre in the Strand, established under the management of John Hollingshead in 1868. This had its chorus of pretty girls, its fantastic costumes and its musical numbers. Most of the productions were taken from France, Germany, and Austrian comic operas translated into English. Hollinghead's successor at the Gaiety in 1886, George Edwardes, altered the tone of burlesque: the costumes became more contemporary and the 'plots' of the musical farces were vaguely contemporary rather than the re-worked old tales of burlesque.

Once again, there was an American influence. In 1884 Minnie Palmer, an American actress, had put on a show called *My Sweetheart*, to great popular acclaim. This was imitated in an English production, *Jack in the Box*, in 1887. Both these productions drew talent from the music halls and from burlesque. They were different from the shows Hollingshead had put on at the Gaiety which had been regarded, according to Raymond Mander and Joe Mitchenson in *Musical Comedy*, as 'bohemian'. The musical comedy of farce was acceptable to a much wider audience.

'George Edwardes's first great success at the Gaity was a musical called *In Town*, which the *Sunday Times* of October 1892 described as 'a curious medley of song, dance and nonsense, with occasional didactic glimmers, sentimental intrusions, and the very vaguest attempts at satirising the modern "masher" [i.e. dandy].' There was tantalizing dancing from Miss Sylvia Grey and comic songs, while leading man Arthur Roberts kept 'the whole house in a roar'.

In 1903 there appeared at the Shaftesbury Theatre an all-black musical from America called *In Dahomey*, of which the theatrical magazine *The Era* said:

Negro entertainments in this country have been associated almost invariably with coon songs, cake-walks and plantation walk arounds. It is therefore really a fresh and novel experiment to introduce to the jaded Londoner an American musical comedy

Hip Hooray
for Coronation
day

that it not only played throughout by real coloured people, but written and composed by clever and able representatives of the Negro race, with lyrics from the pen of a member of the same interesting nationality.

In Dahomey with music composed by Will Marion Cook, who had studied with Anton Dvorak, was, said *The Era*, greeted by an audience which was both 'large and enthusiastic'.

At this period, variety itself was beginning to change, and the shows were taking on the title of 'revue', a term which indicated that a theme, however rough and ready, linked the various parts of the show. Then ragtime arrived from America, and in 1919 the Original Dixieland Jazz Band which was a sensation.

The musical arrived on film with the talkies in the late 1920s and along with adventure films became the most popular entertainment of the 1930s. Musicals of various kinds filled the London stages. And from the early twentieth century, the lines of chorus girls, kicking their legs to a catchy tune, became an essential part of the show. As Mander and Mitchenson point out in *Musical Comedy*, it was American producers who coined the phrase 'Bring on the Girls' to save a flagging performance, just as the great horseman Ducrow was reputed to have exclaimed a century earlier when irritated by spoken drama, 'Cut the cackle and come to the 'osses'.

The attraction of women on stage had been, from the early nineteenth century, one which ran counter to the public morality of the day, especially when they dressed in alluring attire. And when variety theatre was entering its dying days in the 1950s, the last card played by the impresarios was the nude revue. This gave rise to one of the most absurd episodes in London's theatrical history, the politics of the nude pose in the years before the sexual and moral revolution of the 1960s. The London stage had been subject to censorship since 1737, either by the Lord Chamberlain or by the local magistrates and later the London County Council. While the dramatic worth of hippodrama or stage spectaculars was the province of the critic, the wider question of the influence of the stage on public morality was the concern of a much broader body of vigilantes who were especially exercised about the powerful attraction for male audiences of the female form. As Marie Lloyd sang in one of her popular numbers, full of winks and nudges and innuendo: 'Every little movement has a meaning, Every little movement tells a tale . . .'

ABOVE, LEFT AND RIGHT: *Scenes from a typical Gaiety Theatre production in 1903, showing some of the changing fashions. The cakewalk (right) was a forerunner of ragtime, and though at the time it was thought to be an example of a new American intrusion into London entertainment, it had its origins back in 1836, when the Jim Crow song was popular.*

CHAPTER

3

PROFITS AND PRUDERY

THERE HAS NEVER BEEN a time when there has not been some battle going on between London's showbusiness impresarios, its insatiable audiences and those who regard themselves as the guardians of public morality. But no episode in this long and amusing saga was ever so rich in its staging, its cast and its brilliant little sub-plots as the battle over the Empire Theatre, Leicester Square, in the 1890s. This one story contains every issue that rumbled across the London stage in the Victorian period and after: sex, drink, prostitution, popular taste and the profits of showbusiness.

The Empire had opened as a theatre in 1884, staging comic operas, but this enterprise soon failed, and as with so many other attempts to found relatively refined places of entertainment, variety shows were resorted to. In 1887, the Empire became a variety theatre and by the 1890s had gained a very special kind of reputation. It was a great gathering place for a range of people, from aristocrats and colonial officials to 'advanced' clergymen, swells, Bohemians and the milling crowds of the West End. An 1890 description of the Empire from *Harper's New Monthly Magazine* by F. Anstey suggests that just being part of the Empire crowd was as important as the entertainment put on there:

You pass through wide, airy corridors and down stairs, to find yourself in a magnificent theatre, and the stall to which you are shown is wide and luxuriously fitted. Smoking is universal, and a large proportion of the audience promenade the outer circles, or stand in groups before the long refreshment bars which are a prominent feature on every tier. Most of the men are in evening dress, and in the boxes are some ladies, also in evening costume, many of them belonging to what is called good society. The women in other parts of the house are generally pretty obvious members of a class which, so long as it behaves itself with propriety in the building, it would, whatever fanatics may say to the contrary, be neither desirable nor possible to exclude. The most noticeable characteristic of the audience is perhaps the very slight attention it pays to whatever is going on upon the stage.

RIGHT: *A programme for the Empire Theatre of Varieties which in the 1890s was the scene of a fierce battle between what the press called 'prudes on the prowl' and the enthusiastic audience of young men who were excited by the ballet dancers and girls who posed in* tableaux vivants.

THE EMPIRE

HONI SOIT QUI MAL Y PENSE

THEATRE of VARIETIES

HEAVEN'S LIGHT OUR GUIDE

... Stage footmen, more gorgeous in livery, but far meeker of aspect than their brethren in private service, slip a giant card bearing a number into a gilded frame on either side of the proscenium before each item of the programme. The electric bell tings, the lights are raised, the orchestra dashes into a prelude, and the artiste whose 'turn' it is comes on. The main and distinctive feature of the entertainment, however, is the ballet divertissement, for which all else is scarcely more than padding, and these ballets are magnificent enough to satisfy the most insatiate appetite for splendour ... Company after company of girls, in costumes of delicately contrasted tints, march, troop, or gallop down the boards, their burnished armour gleaming and their rich dresses scintillating in the limelight ...

The author of this splendid description of the Empire is himself struck by the grace and beauty of the *première danseuse*:

To see her advance on the points of her toes, her arms curved symmetrically above her head, a smile of innocent childlike delight on her face ... is an experience indeed. Then her high-stepping prance round the stage, her little impulsive runs and bashful retreats, the astonishing complacency with which she submits to being seized and supported in every variety of uncomfortable attitude by the personage next in importance to herself, her final teetotum whirl, are all evidently charged with a deep but mysterious significance.

What concerned the moralists was that the 'deep but mysterious significance' of this apparently innocent display was sex: the Empire exuded it. There were men about town drinking in the music hall promenade, being stimulated by the performance of the girls on stage and solicited by the prostitutes who patrolled the bars. Throughout the Victorian period, actresses were regarded as loose women, and the theatres associated with prostitution. At the Empire the connection was very obvious, and quite blatant. It wasn't the actresses who were 'ladies of the night', but some of the salaciousness of the promenade rubbed off on them.

Everyone knew what the Empire was like; the reputation of its great rival in Leicester Square, the Alhambra, was no different. The manager there had told a Parliamentary Select Committee in 1866 that only about 1 in 100 of his audience were prostitutes, a mere 35 to an audience of 3,500. You simply could not stop these women going into theatres or hanging around them.

The storm at the Empire blew up in 1894 when two innocent American men, part of the West End crowd, took a look in the celebrated music hall and were solicited by prostitutes in the promenade. Outraged, they reported their experience to the leading campaigner against vice, the wonderfully named Mrs Ormiston Chant. She herself decided to take a look a few months later. In evidence to the London County Council's Music Halls and Theatres committee she recorded her shocked impression, not simply of the prostitution in the Empire, but of the provocative nature of the ballets on stage:

To begin with, there was one dancer in flesh coloured tights and I used no opera glasses at first, but at last I had to use them to see whether she even had tights on or not, so nearly was the colour of the flesh imitated. She had nothing on but

RIGHT: *The well-to-do audience at the Empire, Leicester Square in 1894, unconcerned, it seems, by the battle raging over the morality of this splendid theatre of varieties, which had opened in 1887.*

PRUDES ON THE PROWL!

ABOVE: *A cartoon from the* Daily Telegraph *which called those opposed to the Empire Theatre 'Prudes on the Prowl', opposing their efforts to clean the place up and get rid of its risqué performances and the prostitutes who patrolled its promenade.*

a very short skirt – which when she danced and pirouetted flew right up to her head, and left the rest of the body with waist exposed except for a very slight white gauze between the limbs. Also there is one central figure in flesh coloured tights, who wears a light gauzy lacy kind of dress and when she comes to the stage, it is as though the body of a naked woman were simply disguised with a film of lace ... There is also a dancer who dances in black silk tights with a black lace dress, and ... she gathers up all her clothing in the face of the man before whom she is dancing, and stretches up her leg and kicks him upon the crown of his head. I noticed that the audience took these peculiarly objectionable parts very quietly.

Mrs Chant was before the LCC committee to oppose the Empire's application for renewal of its licence. Whereas theatres were licensed by the Lord Chamberlain's office, which concerned itself little with the appearance of dancers and actresses on stage at that time, music halls were faced with a much more vigilant and prudish authority. The London County Council had come into being in 1889, and was led by 'Progressives' who were, in many ways, great social reformers, but of the most humourless and puritanical kind. In their administration of music and dancing licences they were especially strict.

The Empire was such a fashionable place that it won a great deal of support from fun-loving West End society, and in the Press. The *Daily Telegraph* ran the story in full, giving great prominence to the proceedings of the licensing committee. Its letters pages raged with argument under the heading 'Prudes on the prowl'. According to Charles Stuart and A.J. Park in their classic history of music hall, *The Variety Stage*, published the year after Mrs Chant's attack on the Empire:

The majority of the press and the public ... sided with the Empire management, and Mrs Chant and her friends came in for a considerable amount of popular opprobrium. The comic papers made abundant capital out of the subject, and this worthy lady, whose conduct, however ill-advised, was undoubtedly inspired by the worthiest motives, found herself satirised in the form of grotesque pictorial sketches, rhyming lampoons, and ... had the distinction of figuring as one of the principal 'guys' of the year.

The LCC decided it would renew the Empire's licence only if a screen were put up between the promenade and the back row of the dress circle and the upper circle, and the sale of drink banned from the

BELOW AND RIGHT: *Ballet girls, whose skin-tight, flesh-coloured leggings made them look naked, aroused the anger of moral reformers opposed to the Empire, Leicester Square, as much as the prostitutes who patrolled the theatre's promenade.*

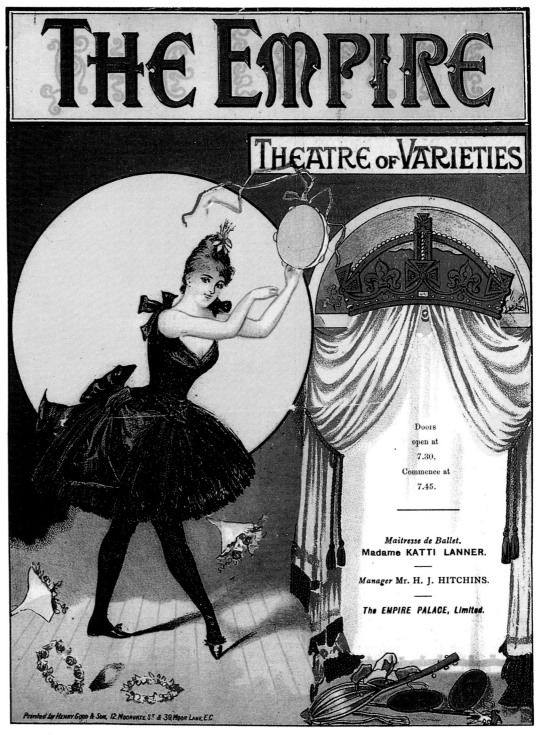

auditorium. George Edwardes, manager of the Empire, protested strongly that this would greatly reduce his profits and the dividend he could pay to his shareholders, and that it was unfair if similar establishments were not forced to do the same.

In October 1894, Edwardes announced to a furious crowd that the Empire would close. On 3 November, it was re-opened with a temporary screen put up. What followed next was described in the *Pall Mall Gazette* of 5 November:

The bar at the back had been shut off from the promenade by means of a screen of woodwork covered with canvas . . . gradually the crowd began to attack the screen. Well dressed men – some of them almost middle-aged – kicked at it from within, burst the canvas, but hardly affecting the woodwork. The attendants – most of whom might have played the giant in a country show – watched in helpless and amused inactivity. Finally there was an attack on the canvas, which was torn away in strips, and passed throughout the crowd, every one endeavouring to secure a scrap of it as a souvenir. Mr Hitchens, the manager, attempted argumentative remonstrance, but was carried away by half a dozen enthusiasts. Then the woodwork of the screen was demolished by vigorous kicks from both sides. The crowd had already cheered itself hoarse, and now began to go out into London, brandishing fragments of the screen . . .

One of the young men who helped pull down the screen at the Empire was Winston Churchill.

The Empire was an extremely profitable business, quoted on the stock exchange, and employing 670 people. When the Palace Theatre – built as an opera house – applied in 1892 for a licence as a music hall, the directors of the Empire opposed it, arguing that such competition would interfere with their '70 per cent' profit. Obviously, the managers of variety theatres had to steer a very careful line between providing the kind of titillating entertainment that drew the crowds and avoiding offence to the authorities, who might take away their licence and their livelihood. In the case of the Empire, the scantily clad dancing girls and the prowling women of the town were profitable, but in other variety theatres which looked to attract a more respectable audience, they were not. By the Edwardian era the Empire was on its way out. A variety impresario like Sir Oswald Stoll, who opened the Coliseum in 1904, would have nothing dubious in his shows. By this time, however, the high-kicking chorus girls who might have made a

RIGHT: *The great rival to the Empire was the Palace Theatre of Varieties in Cambridge Circus which had been built as the Royal English Opera in 1891, but had failed and was taken over by variety in 1892.*

RIGHT: *A cartoon making fun of the demand that the Empire Theatre should put up a screen between the theatre's promenade and the stage. The joke is that the 'living picture' of apparently nude women on stage has been obscured by the demands of the moral reformer, the redoubtable Mrs Ormiston Chant.*

Victorian lady blush were no longer regarded as morally doubtful. Both performances and public attitudes changed, and 'family' entertainment became more profitable than the bohemian shows of the Alhambra or the Empire.

It was the nude show, however, that kept the old variety theatres going in their dying days of the 1950s, when they had lost most of their family audience to the cinema, and were about to lose it entirely to television. This last tragi-comic episode began during the Second World War when nude shows became popular amongst the servicemen in London. After the war, as variety continued to lose its appeal, some showmen began to introduce nudes into the performance, and eventually to bring in nude revues in which the other acts were padding. Paul Raymond, who had a mind-reading act in variety, got into management and went on tour with a show called Vaudeville Express in the early 1950s. On the second circuit of variety theatres, it was doing badly when it was suggested to him that nudity was a crowd-puller. If the family audience had gone, there was a market for single men in search of sexual titillation, as there always is.

Although the mainstream of popular entertainment could not countenance even simulated nudity, *real* nudity was more lucrative than the out-dated variety acts. Paul Raymond recalls:

I was running my own variety show called Vaudeville Express and because it was my show I put myself as top of the bill. ... Things were very bad in those times, even worse than they are now, and we got a booking at the Queen's Park Hippodrome in Manchester and the guy quite rightly said, 'Well, there's no point in your bringing your show here, we must have nudes in the show'. There were two girls in those days on the variety bill and they would open the show with a tap dance and open the second half with a tap dance, and I offered them an extra 10 shillings a week to show their boobs three times – one in the first half, another one in the first half and one was a double act in the second half. So the guy said, 'fine' and from Vaudeville Express it became the Festival of the Nudes. All of a sudden the takings went probably double what they were before. I was clever enough to realize that I was not the star of the show – it was the girls.

These were modest beginnings. In time an important element of any show became the total nude. But this was a very difficult and delicate act to perform, for over the years rules had been evolved by the Lord

Chamberlain's office for the presentation of nudes in theatres. Exactly how, when and why these rules came about nobody seems to know, for the Lord Chamberlain's men were, historically, amateur censors whose own grasp of the rules they were supposed to be administering were very shaky indeed, as their evidence to a great many House of Commons committees demonstrates.

The effect of the rule about absolute nudity was, however, that the lady (no rules existed for men) should be absolutely static. Broadly speaking, the more women pranced around on stage, the more they had to wear; or at least, the less they could reveal of their bodies. The ultimate solution was the 'fan dance' in which the audience could not tell whether or not the performer *was* nude, so dextrous was the wristy whirring of the ostrich feathers. It was hard work. Sandra Barnham was a seasoned exponent of this very difficult illusion:

The fan dance was one of my favourite dances, it was so balletic you could get carried away – it was a beautiful feeling. But to learn it was damn hard work – I mean our hands used to swell up in rehearsals because the fans were so heavy and there's a certain way of spreading your fan and holding it wide and your thumbs used to swell up . . . So to learn it, yes, was hard, but it was worth it. It was timed perfectly so that you had two girls with you, so if you took your fans away the girls would cover you. Never – until the last minute – did you ever see the slightest inkling which was when the tabs closed and which was for about ten seconds.

Where a performer was obviously nude the rules were, according to a note provided by the Lord Chamberlain's office to a 1966 committee:

Actresses may pose completely nude provided the pose is motionless and expressionless; the pose is artistic and something rather more than a display of nakedness; and the lighting must be subdued. Striptease as such is not allowed in a stage play.

There were many ways round this bizarre ruling: the nude might not move a muscle, but somehow she would be moved. Marie Authie is a veteran of the variety nude revues:

Although the Lord Chamberlain said that nudes musn't move, we got over that by letting our props move. For instance, I would be in a sledge pulled by two girls dressed as reindeer and the sledge would move but I didn't. And then, of course, the next scene would

RIGHT: *A classic 1950s nude show number, the fan dance, in which the performer could move around freely while not revealing her nudity, then posed naked briefly at the end, while remaining absolutely still.*

FAR RIGHT: *In the 1950s, variety theatres which were losing their audiences made a last-ditch attempt to survive with nude shows, such as* Paree for Me. *Other titles included* Strip Strip Hooray, *and* See Nipples and Die.

be the Rock of Ages with the girl clinging to a cross on a rock with a wind machine blowing her hair, blowing the tulle: they moved but she still didn't move. And then there was the Queen of the Jungle – with me in the centre with a spear, with a stuffed tiger, holding the hand of a little chimp. Which was fine at the beginning of the tour, but after six months of hard knocks the chimp was beginning to look a little bit deflated. One night I just happened to gaze down – I

could move my eyes, mind you – I gazed down and there was a big mound of sawdust coming from Charlie Chimp. So I was left standing holding a deflated balloon trying not to giggle.

Theatre historian Michael Booth, who was a postgraduate student in London in the 1950s, recalls a classic instance of a nude running rings around the Lord Chamberlain's rules:

I remember going to Collins' Music Hall in Islington about 1957 and seeing Peaches Page who had just achieved some notoriety at the Windmill Theatre because she had been prosecuted by the Lord Chamberlain for running across the stage when she saw a mouse, which was against the law. In Islington she played the part of Jack in a tableau vivant of Jack and the Beanstalk. And when the

RIGHT: *Three classic 'living pictures', in which girls dressed in skin-tight costumes appeared, from a distance and with subtle lighting, to be naked. These* tableaux vivants *were a favourite at the Palace Theatre of Varieties in Cambridge Circus, and the management always claimed 'artistic' merit for them, as they often depicted famous pictures which happened to have nudes in them.*

LEFT: *A cartoon of two gentleman on their way to see apparently nude ladies posing in* tableaux vivants. *One says: 'Have you your opera glasses?' The other replies: 'No, but I've got a telescope.'*

curtain went up you saw the bean stalk and Peaches Page clinging [to it]. She was wearing a green hat with a green feather in it, she was wearing green boots and she was really wearing nothing else. The bean stalk, which was a rope dressed up, was being pulled into the flies and spinning madly: she was rotating all over the place. You could see every part of her anatomy quite distinctly but she didn't move a muscle, thus fulfilling the very letter of the law.

The game of 'now you see me, now you don't' had been played out over many years, in different ways. From the early nineteenth century, apparently nude performers – like those that had upset Mrs Ormiston Chant at the Empire – had been appearing somewhere on the London stage. In the 1830s they had been a feature of the Coal Hole, a forerunner of music hall, in the Strand. They wore skin-tight costumes, so that from a distance they appeared to be naked. Typically, single figures or groups would form *tableaux vivants*, or living pictures, also known as *poses plastiques*.

Very often they depicted a well-known painting, which just happened to include a group of naked damsels draped in thin silk. Or they would be made up to look like a stone statue. This was a favourite form of entertainment at the Palace Theatre. In a typically Victorian way, the fiction that this was really art rather than simple voyeurism was generally maintained just as the dress of ballet dancers, which many men found exciting, was justified on the grounds of artistic expression.

In the 1950s nude shows, with such titles as *See Nipples and Die*, the same argument was used, but by then the pretence had worn pretty thin. The experience of those who performed in these shows is now both sad and laughable.

One of the most famous places in London, at which these shows were the standard bill of fare, was the Windmill Theatre, on the border of Soho and Piccadilly Circus. Opened in 1931, the Windmill soon took to nude reviews. Sandra Barnham performed there:

Audiences at the 'Mill were very good – we used to get good applause when we did good dance numbers – and very appreciative. There was always a sign saying you weren't allowed to have binoculars as you walked in, so they were aware of the fact that you weren't. But you'd always get the odd one who would try and we'd be on stage and you'd probably see somebody with binoculars and then you'd get to the side of the stage and say to the stage manager,

ABOVE: *A London institution between 1932 and its closure in 1964 was the Windmill, which ran a daily programme of non-stop variety from 2.30 pm to 11 pm, in which the most important features were the girls, dancers and nude posers. During the last War it had the slogan 'We never closed' – it kept going right through the Blitz.*

'Third row down, second one in – binoculars'. And before you even got off the stage you'd see an usherette come through, bang him on the shoulder and his binoculars would disappear and he'd sit there very meek and mild and embarrassed . . .

And also another funny thing that used to happen: it was always the end of the fan dance and probably the front row had seen it about three times and decided to leave – but they'd never walk round . . . you'd get them climbing over the seats. And the back row – they would climb forward so they got nearer to the front to be nearer the girls! So they used to take turns!

Over the thirty years in which the Windmill functioned it had a most peculiar place in London entertainment, and an odd relationship with the Lord Chamberlain's office. Strictly speaking, unless what was performed there could be regarded as a stage play, the Lord Chamberlain had no jurisdiction over it; the variety theatre licence was with the LCC and later the Greater London Council. In 1941, Vivian Van Damm, manager of the Windmill, wrote to the Lord Chamberlain's office to ask if the revues put on at the theatre – stand up comics, sketches, and nude *tableaux* – should really be regarded as variety. The answer he received, according to the book by the last Comptroller of the Lord Chamberlain's office, Lt. Col. Sir John Johnston, was a classic piece of waffle. In *The Lord Chamberlain's Blue Pencil*, Johnston quotes the then Secretary to the Lord Chamberlain's Office, aptly called George Titman, as replying:

Either you must continue to run your 'Revuedeville' as a stage play as heretofore and conform to the Lord Chamberlain's requirement of which you are well aware; or you must change it to 'Varietyville' by entirely separating the various acts and eliminating any idea of a theme running through the show.

Van Damm stayed with the Lord Chamberlain, a much softer censor as a rule than the London County Council, and, as John Johnston records, 'There was seldom a shortage of volunteers from the Lord Chamberlain's office to pay visits from time to time to check the comics were sticking to their gags which had been licensed and that the nudes were complying with theirs.'

In 1968, the old system of censorship was abolished and those putting on any kind of public show were left at the mercy of public opinion and the law courts. There was, for a time, a flowering of nudity, as

ABOVE: *Prostitutes congregated around the theatres in London, tainting actresses unjustifiably. This is an illustration from Henry Mayhew's survey of London people, showing prostitutes – identified by their hooped petticoats – in the Haymarket.*

LEFT: *We do not normally today regard ballet dancers as sexy, but in the Victorian and Edwardian periods their costume was regarded as arousing, as it revealed their legs and even more of their anatomy when their skirts flew up in the air.*

in the *Living Theatre* at the Round House Theatre in Chalk Farm, housed in the beehive-shaped building of an old railway turntable, or the production *Oh Calcutta* – a pun on the French *quel cul tu as*, or 'what a backside you have'. Since then, however, there has been little trouble on stage, and the sex shows have retreated to a few sordid dives in Soho, to private parties or the internationally popular Raymond's Revue Bar, opened in 1958 and still going, in which girls reveal their genitals to a silent, transfixed audience of Japanese businessmen and other tourists in a small theatre of computerized lighting and pounding popular music, with none of the opulence or socializing of the Empire, Leicester Square, in its heyday.

Although Soho still has a reputation as London's central red light district, practically nothing remains of the rich world of pornography and prostitution which thrived in the Victorian era. As the Canadian historian Tracy C. Davis has pointed out in her brilliant study of women and erotica in nineteenth-century London, *Actresses as Working Women*, the relationship between theatres and music halls, and the torrid world of sleazy, night-time London was very close.

In the mid- to late-nineteenth century, the focus of low life and prostitution extended much further afield than Soho. The centre was the Strand, between the newly created gentlemen's clubs in the Pall Mall area and the City, and linking many theatres and prototype music halls in the 1850s, such as the Coal Hole, the Cyder Cellars and Evans's.

Davis paints a vivid picture of men drawn to the area, excited by girls on stage kicking their legs in the air and revealing their underwear, tumbling out into the streets teeming with prostitutes where pornography, chiefly of actresses in various states of undress, was freely on sale. The West End stage, viewed from this perspective, is a stimulant to what the prudes regarded as immorality: it is all of a piece with its hinterland of dirty bookshops, selling such salacious publications as *The Day's Doings*, and brothels.

What went on on stage was not, by contemporary standards, obscene for the most part, nor was it necessarily regarded consciously as such in the Victorian and Edwardian periods. But in retrospect, it is possible to see how the most innocent-looking ballet dancer in tights and tutu, the most rosily jolly principal boy played by a woman wearing high boots and tight-fitting leggings, and even the popular male impersonators of the music halls, such as Vesta Tilly and Ella Shields, because the contours of their limbs were revealed by their costumes, could be regarded as the sex symbols of their day.

Certainly Mrs Ormiston Chant felt that the problem was not so much what you wore if you were a woman, as the way that you wore it. In defence of her position she was quoted in the *Daily Telegraph* of 18 October 1894 as saying:

Do I object to ballet? Nothing is further from my mind. I don't object to tights, as such. I know that when you dance very vigorously you must not be impeded by clinging petticoats about your ankles, or

LEFT: *Shops selling pornography in the districts where there were many theatres – at the back of the Strand and later near Leicester Square – offered pictures of 'actresses' in compromising poses encouraging the view that they were all prostitutes.*

even about the knees. If need be, I think I could devise a costume which would give this freeness and yet clothe the limbs, although I am not one of those who think it a shame to have legs. It is the motive at the back of it all . . . which makes the thing evil.

The context in which simulated nudity, or any kind of female dress which exposed parts of the body normally concealed, was displayed, was significant. Cross-dressing – women as men and men as women – was an established feature of pantomime, and was generally acceptable. So too, in time, was ballet dress. And from the time the Gaiety Theatre was opened in 1868 right through the Victorian and Edwardian periods, the inter-war years, and the arrival of commercial television and *Sunday Night at the London Palladium*, the chorus line of leggy girls, arms linked, legs kicking high to reveal under-clothing, has been considered 'family' entertainment.

A version of this kind of performance, first imported to London from France in the mid-nineteenth century, was, on occasion, regarded as over the top. This was the cancan. It originated in Paris as a communal dance, performed by both men and women, with the characteristic high kick, and the leg held high and twirled about. The first performance in London was in 1866 at the Princess's Theatre, and the performers were four *men* imported from Paris. The resourceful John Hollingshead, then stage director of the Alhambra music hall, brought over a Parisian dancer Finette in 1867 with her version of the cancan, in which she dressed as a man. Hollingshead arranged for her to perform first at the Lyceum Theatre, to gain respectability, before putting her on at the Alhambra in 1868, where she was a sensation. Her high kicking was known to the French as *le présentez-armes*.

In *My Lifetime*, John Hollingshead gives his reasons for trying out the cancan first at a theatre:

I only knew the can-can as the daughter of the 'Carmagnole' the favourite dance of the Great Revolution, but I knew that in England – the country with a dozen licensing systems and only one fish-sauce – where names excite more horror than things, that the can-can was not a welcome sound to the licensing authorities. . . . knowing that Mr. E. T. Smith was running a pantomime at the Lyceum Theatre, written by Mr. W. S. Gilbert (later of Gilbert and Sullivan fame) and knowing that Mr. Milano had 'arranged' the dances for this pantomime, I thought that it would be prudent to get the Lord Chamberlain's stamp on Finette before we took her to

ABOVE AND RIGHT: *The dress of girls playing 'principal boys' in pantomime was regarded as sexually alluring in the Victorian and Edwardian periods when, in everyday life, women never wore trousers. Stage costume, much more revealing than anything acceptable in everyday life, was in general thought to be titillating.*

BELOW: *The high-kicking French dancer Finette was one of the first performers of the sensational cancan in London in 1868. At this time the dance was not associated with frilly dresses and knickers. In fact the first performers of the dance in London were men, and later performers included women dressed as men.*

the debatable ground of Leicester Square … Finette, duly stamped with the legitimate stamp, after the Lyceum pantomime was over, appeared at the Alhambra and made a success. She was dressed as effectively as and a little more decently than a 'burlesque prince' and her dance had none of the offensive features of the can-can in petticoats. The most that could be said against it was that it was not a hornpipe.

The very same technique of getting the Lord Chamberlain's stamp of approval on contentious material was used by Paul Raymond in the 1950s. He submitted photographs of the poses of naked girls and various tableaux to the Lord Chamberlain who would mark them with a blue pencil, approved or not, or approved with certain conditions such as 'only in subdued lighting'. He could then take his seal of approval to the provinces.

The Lord Chamberlain's office was generally regarded as a soft touch on this kind of thing, for its main purpose in reading plays was to examine text for offensive references to Royalty, leading figures, foreign dignitaries and for spoken obscenity and blasphemy.

Rivalry between West End music halls produced some of the most amusing and revealing controversies over public taste. The Palace Theatre, in Cambridge Circus, became a variety theatre in 1892. Because it was built after the London County Council began to license such places, the local authority had a greater say in the way it was run than it had with the Empire, Leicester Square. The Palace naturally wanted to incorporate the kind of promenade that caused such a fuss at the Empire, but the LCC refused permission. As a rival attraction, in 1893 the Palace specialized in *tableaux vivants* with women imitating nineteenth-century paintings, lying around on stage apparently naked in skin-tight *maillots*. The artistic pretention allowed the Palace to get away with what was blatant sale of sex, though a National Vigilance campaigner noticed a wrinkle or two in 'Ariadne', a depiction of Johann Dannecker's sculpture:

'Ariadne'… so far as I can put it into language, represents a naked woman lying on the back of a lion. There were four or five wrinkles on the lower parts of the limb, distinguishing it from an ordinary picture. The left leg was placed under the lower part of the right leg, producing these wrinkles. She was lying in such a position that had it not been for the tights gross indecency would have been the result.

RIGHT: *The Gaiety Theatre in the Strand was famous for its attractive dancers, who would often be dressed as men. This, in the context of the time, was especially alluring as it revealed their figures.*

The LCC ruling was that these clothed but apparently nude models should have a wisp of some material over the loins, and advised that it was for the spectators to bear in mind that, though the women looked nude, they were not really: it was a matter of 'inference and faith' rather than 'observation and knowledge'.

The question of drink

Just as the moralists and licensing authorities sought to subdue the sexual allure of dancing girls and *tableaux vivants*, so they made a concerted attack on drinking in music halls. Newly opened variety theatres could not get a licence to sell drink in the auditorium, and were designed with theatre seating. The big music hall syndicates could survive a fall in refreshment receipts as the money taken at the door had become a high proportion of their earnings. A great many of the smaller music halls closed down in this period.

ABOVE: *A temperance meeting at Sadler's Wells Theatre in 1854, signing the teetotal pledge. The opponents of drink were anti-music hall and anti-theatre.*

From their earliest years, the music halls had been dogged by the social reformers and moralists because they were there to sell alcoholic drinks. The temperance movement, which arose in the early nineteenth century to oppose the drinking of spirits and reinstate the health-giving qualities of beer, became a considerable force in the late nineteenth century, by which time it opposed all alcohol. There were mass signings of the teetotal pledge in London theatres and halls.

Those who opposed the music halls contended that they encouraged drinking, although there was a good deal of evidence that they did the opposite. A man having a drink with his wife or girlfriend while watching a few variety turns remained more sober than if he had spent the night in a gin palace doing nothing but drink in male company. However, drink was absolutely critical to the finances of music halls, as many witnesses made clear to the House of Commons Select Committee on Theatres and Music Halls in 1892. It was the refreshment receipts that made the music halls much more lucrative than

the theatres, and the main reason why they attracted big investment funds in the 1880s and 1890s. This was why the theatres were so fiercely opposed to music halls being allowed to stage drama, for it was feared that they would lose their audience to the more congenial alcoholic and smoky atmosphere of these glorified pubs.

In his evidence to the Select Committee of 1892, the actor Henry Irving was asked if he thought a drama put on where smoking and drinking in the auditorium were allowed would damage his trade. He replied, 'I think there is no doubt about that; as Mr Bolton said, if I were playing the *Corsican Brothers* and a theatre was playing it next door, with the advantages of smoking and drinking, my theatre would be empty, and I should have to do something else . . .' Irving said he believed 'the music halls want to swallow the theatres wholesale to further their custom as publicans'.

Irving was not opposed to drink: he made the point that the public houses around the theatres in which he played had their custom swelled by his audiences. He had no objection to music hall, which he went to on occasion and enjoyed. But as an actor-manager he did not want to have to compete with the big business of the halls.

While the theatres fought successfully to keep drink and drama apart, the temperance movement inspired a number of enterprises intended to provide an alcohol-free alternative to the public house and the music hall. In the 1880s, attempts were made to set up coffee taverns with music and dancing licences: nine were in existence in London in 1892. One of these was the Victoria Theatre (now the Old Vic), which was converted into a temperance music hall for a time by Emma Conn. All these enterprises failed, not simply because they lacked the income from alcoholic drinks, but because they tended to have a pious and unattractive atmosphere. The same was true of the People's Palace created in the Mile End Road, East London, built by social reformers inspired by the novel by Walter Besant in which a young heiress just down from Cambridge goes to live as a seamstress among the poor and is moved to invest some of her fortune in such a place. Queen Victoria herself opened the first phase of the ambitious building in 1887, but the People's Palace was confused in its aims between education and recreation. It became part of London University in 1907.

The one enduring enterprise of the social reformers and what has been dubbed 'rational recreation' – the provision by the well-to-do of worthwhile amusements for the people – was the working men's club movement. This grew out of various philanthropic schemes in the

LEFT: *In the 1890s, the Victoria Theatre – now the Old Vic – was turned into a temperance music hall which sold no alcoholic drink, but attempted to provide all the other pleasures of this popular form of entertainment. It was not a success.*

1840s which culminated in 1862 in the creation of the Working Men's Club and Institute Union – the CIU, for short. Its influential members included such people as the Reverend Henry Solly, a temperance reformer and teetotaller, and former Unitarian minister. To begin with, alcoholic drinks were banned and there was an evangelical air about the movement; the Notting Hill Workman's Hall even had a working model of the Eddystone lighthouse outside for those who saw the light and abandoned the pub for the club.

Among its vice-presidents and benefactors in the early days, the CIU could list a veritable army of Right Honourable Dukes, Earls and minor Lords. The gentry put up the money or gave buildings or pieces of land, while the reformers got on with the practical task of creating the right kind of alcohol-free, uplifting entertainment. Octavia Hill, the housing reformer, founded the Barrett Court Club in a slum district of Marylebone as an addition to the philanthropic housing scheme she ran. To keep the locals away from the public house she first tried to buy it, and when this failed she opposed the licence of the Duke of Walmer and had it closed down. In its place, she founded a Temperance Association called the Blue Order of the Sons of Phoenix. Her idea of a bit of fun was revealed in a letter she wrote in 1873:

> *There is a kind of piano at the Club; we shall want plenty of song. Probably you know the kind; simple ones, that will do them real good, and especially 'Angels ever bright and fair'.*

Within a few years, the CIU was losing its grip on the clubs and having to swallow *some* drink, and some more diverting entertainment. By the 1880s, most were in the process of throwing off the burden of their philanthropic founders and their rules, installing stages, bringing in music hall acts and generally enjoying themselves. They had discovered that by opening a bar and selling drinks they could become financially self-sufficient: they had no need of prudish patrons.

In the 1890s, working men's clubs were putting on quite lavish entertainments and operating like small, members-only music halls. When variety theatres went out of business, these clubs provided a haven for some of the artists, as well as an enthusiastic clientele for strippers when the police closed down most Soho clubs in the 1960s.

If the temperance working men's clubs became more like music halls, the music halls themselves had become more like theatres – tables and chairs were replaced by seating arranged as stalls, circle, gallery and so on – and those who ran the largest in London, such as

ABOVE: *One of the many worthy failures of the temperance movement to provide alternative 'rational recreation' for the masses was the People's Palace in the Mile End Road, founded by the writer and reformer Walter Besant. Queen Victoria opened it in 1887, but it was never completed and eventually became part of London University.*

ABOVE: *The People's Palace on its opening day. The grand Queen's Hall never became the resort of poor East Enders that its founders had hoped.*

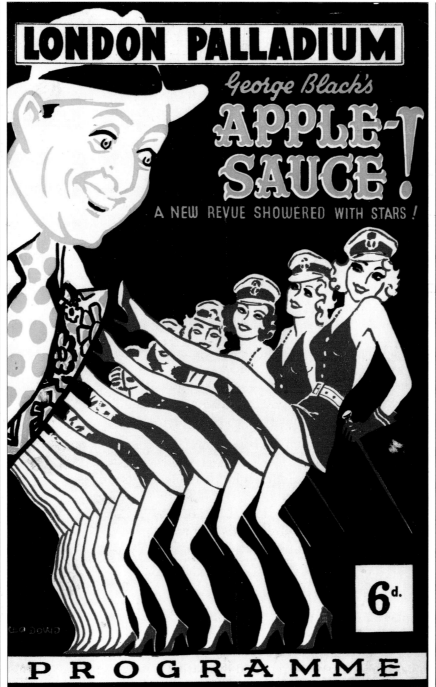

LEFT: *The naughty side of music hall was exemplified by such stars as Max Miller, billed here at the Palladium in 1941 along with the essential line of chorus girls.*

Oswald Stoll at the Coliseum, sought respectability as well as handsome profits, putting the public house image behind them. They received their reward in 1912 with the first ever Royal Variety Command Performance at the Palace Theatre.

The exclusion of Marie Lloyd from the bill was indicative of the way in which 'vulgarity' had been expunged from these West End variety theatres. In her performances she represented something of the old spirit of music hall, which she had learned in Hoxton as a young girl, going to the Grecian in City Road where her father worked part-time as a waiter. Her songs were, in her heyday as the most celebrated female music hall artiste, full of *double entendres*, and she was usually pictured winking one eye. It might have been that reputation that led to her exclusion from the Royal Variety performance, or her personal life – she was going through a very public divorce at the time.

It is very difficult now to disentangle fact from fiction in accounts of Marie Lloyd's performances. There is a story, almost certainly apocryphal, that she was summoned to sing her songs to the LCC Theatre and Music Hall Committee. She sang them straight, and nobody could see any offence in them. Then she sang 'Come into the Garden, Maude' with lots of winks and lewd gestures to prove her point that the mode of performance was what made the difference. There are stories that she appeared on stage with an umbrella, and after struggling to open it said, 'Oh, what a relief, I haven't had it up for ages'. She is also alleged to have sung a song beginning 'She sits amongst the cabbages and peas …', to cries of shame from Mrs Ormiston Chant. But many students of music hall deny that was ever in her repertoire.

One point that is probably true is that she would be much *more* restrained in her performances in the East End than in the West End. It was an accepted view of the Select Committee of 1892 that the further East you went in London, the less acceptable any kind of naughtiness was. The implication was that the bohemian West End of London was where sexual innuendo was most applauded. No doubt Marie Lloyd varied her performances a good deal, and they could be rude. But the risqué performers were a very minor part of music hall and variety.

When silent cinema arrived and began rapidly to gather a substantial audience in the early 1900s, licensing authorities and the promoters of the new entertainment were faced with some novel problems. There was great concern that the darkened auditorium would be a den of vice – which to some extent it became – and that there would be no control over the material shown in cinemas. Faced

with the prospect of licensing authorities all over the country deciding individually what to ban and what to allow, the film industry set up in 1912 its own system of self-policing, the British Board of Film Censors, with G.A. Redford, a former reader of plays from the Lord Chamberlain's office, as its first President.

Local authorities could still, if they wanted, censor films in their own area, and some did on occasions. But, by and large, the judgement of the film censors was accepted in the 1930s. This is not surprising as the forty-three censorship rules devised in 1917 outlawed depictions of prostitution, premarital and extramarital sex, sexual perversion, incest, seduction, nudity, venereal disease, orgies, swearing, abortion, brothels and white slavery among thirty-three items dealing generally with morality. Even so, local cinema managers had to be on their guard against moral campaigners.

There was perpetual concern about the effect films might have on children and the mass audience which was regarded as especially impressionable. In fact, nothing was shown in cinemas anything like as daring as what has for some years now been seen on television. At the same time, alcoholic drink was never allowed in cinemas, despite the fact that the super-cinemas of the Thirties included cafés. Smoking, however, was universal, producing that romantic milky beam of the projector in the darkened auditorium.

There is no doubt that during the century from the 1830s to the 1930s public entertainment became more respectable, less dependent on strong drink, and was enjoyed in infinitely more salubrious surroundings. And as entertainment moved into the home, with the advent of radio and television, the heady days of the Empire and its promenade, the ripping-down of screens and the fierce opposition of Mrs Ormiston Chant were long forgotten.

It was not so much that the temperance movement and the moralists had won as that the showmen who promoted mass entertainment had done their job for them. Generally speaking, the larger an audience is the less acceptable any kind of morally dubious performance: mass entertainment and morality tend to go hand in hand. The battles of the Victorian and Edwardian periods may appear quaint to us, but they had a great influence on the way later entertainment developed. And just as there was a struggle to control what was permissible on stage, a battle was fought out in theatre auditoria to control the behaviour of the audience, and to create the kind of refined ambiance we expect of West End theatres today.

LEFT: *The legendary Marie Lloyd, whose real performance is now shrouded in myth. Did she really sing a song with the line 'She sits among the cabbages and peas'? Did she really struggle to open her umbrella on stage and remark: 'I haven't had it up for ages.'?*

ABOVE: *Though there was great concern about the morality of films from Hollywood, cinemas themselves were very respectable places of entertainment, which did not serve alcohol, though many of the super-cinemas of the 1930s had their own cafés.*

CHAPTER 4

THE SILENT CHOCOLATE

T O SIT IN THE AUDIENCE of a West End theatre is, for all but the most seasoned playgoer, a special experience. There is an overwhelming feeling of occasion, of the need to behave properly, to dress up – though that is less *de rigueur* than it was a few years ago – to remain silent through the most exciting of scenes, in fact to show no emotion at all, except laughter in a comedy, until the time comes for a round of applause.

For quite a few people, this atmosphere is off-putting. It sets up a kind of emotional vertigo, a terror that, carried away by the drama, you might blurt something out and in doing so disgrace yourself. This is especially true of 'serious' theatre, a play by Henrik Ibsen perhaps, where the characters on stage endure the most heart-rending torments while the audience remains implacable, responding with only a communal gasp at the terrifying crack of a pistol as it breaks the reverential silence. Only in pantomime, which survives around Christmas time as an amusement for children, is it acceptable for the audience to get involved, shouting 'Look out' or 'Oh no she isn't'.

The ultimate theatrical paranoia arrived in the 1930s when Cadburys devised the 'silent' chocolate box for starving playgoers who had to have some sustenance during the performance but were fearful of breaking the silence with the rustle of paper. According to Cadburys' promotions at the time, the idea had been suggested by the actress Sybil Thorndike who had been put out, no doubt, by irritating rustles reaching the stage.

It has not always been like that in London theatres. At times they could be as rowdy as a football match, and one of the great pleasures was the opportunity to shout to the performers and let off steam. Even within living memory, there were theatres with quite different codes of behaviour from those modern audiences are familiar with. Ivy Groom recalls the last days of East End melodrama with its evil villains, its heroes and heroines:

During the interval they used to go outside, those that wanted to go outside, to the fish shop on the other side of the road. Well when the

ABOVE: *It was the great size of London, and the improvement in transport, that first gave rise to the dominance of West End in the nineteenth century. Its Theatreland – advertised here on a London Underground poster – had by the 1920s become a playground for the middle classes.*

The behaviour of theatre, and later music hall, audiences, became more and more restrained in the Victorian era, creating the stultifying atmosphere of the modern West End theatre.

RIGHT: *Pantomime audiences could be less well-behaved, and even these middle-class youngsters pictured here at Drury Lane in the 1890s would have had a chance to make a noise and communicate with the actors on stage.*

FAR RIGHT: *The ultimate paranoia of refined theatre – the rustle of chocolate papers – led Cadburys in the 1930s to offer a solution. It is not clear if the 'silent chocolate' had a waxy, non-rustle wrapper, or no wrapper at all, but no doubt it was a life-saver for thousands of starving playgoers.*

Sh·h·h !

ANOTHER DISTURBER OF THE PIECE!

And he could so easily have avoided this by getting one of the new "silent" boxes of Cadbury's Chocolates. No rustling of paper wrappings, no crackling of foil, no pained rebukes from his neighbours. This box of "Princess Elizabeth" Chocolates is so ingeniously devised that, though its contents are amply protected, they are unpacked in decorous silence. Bear this in mind next time you visit a theatre or cinema.

ASK AT THE THEATRE FOR THE NEW "SILENT" BOX OF

CADBURY'S

Princess Elizabeth

CHOCOLATES - 2/6 per ½ lb. box

interval was over and it was time for them to come in, if they hadn't finished their fish and chips they'd come in and finish them inside; and all the wrapping they had they screwed up in balls to pelt the one that they didn't like, which naturally was the villain. So they used to pelt him with all the scraps of paper that they fetched in from outside. But that made the show really, because they laughed; they liked that, you see. They liked it ...

The evolution of polite theatre came about bit by bit during the Victorian period; once cinema and the variety theatres had taken away the mass audience, it became almost the only surviving form.

ABOVE: *Cheap catering for the masses – fish and chip shops, Lyons corner houses and other chains – was a great challenge to the public house. As these establishments did not serve alcohol they contributed to the sharp decline in drinking in the twentieth century.*

The rise of respectable theatre

One of the great differences in the experience of London entertainment in the nineteenth century was between the relaxed atmosphere of the music halls, in which you could smoke, eat and drink, and that of the West End theatres in which eating and drinking were officially outlawed. All generalizations about audience behaviour are likely to be misleading, for the atmosphere could change under different managements. East End and other local theatres kept the old tradition of eating and drinking alive until the end of the century, and even into the 1920s. Their more robust audiences defied the official regulations which the Lord Chamberlain's office imposed on places with a theatrical licence, and enjoyed their drama with a good helping of pies, sandwiches and ale. This was also true of West End theatres until about the 1860s; you could count on some refreshment even in theatres like Drury Lane. In *The Drama of Yesterday and Today*, the critic Clement Scott described that theatre in 1849 as having 'very little luxury, no lounge stalls, the pit right up to the orchestra, the faithful pitites sitting on hard benches and constantly disturbed between the acts by women with huge and clumsy baskets filled with apples, oranges, nuts, ginger beer bottles, stout and bills of the play'.

The pit was that area of the theatre at ground-floor level immediately below the stage which was later taken over by the stalls. And the 'pitites' to whom Scott refers were regarded in the first half of the nineteenth century and beyond as the most critical, best informed and most socially mixed part of the audience. In the boxes were the relatively well-to-do, and in the gallery the soldiers, sailors, domestic servants and others who could only afford a place in the 'gods'. The saying 'playing to the gallery' still refers, snobbishly, to an appeal to the coarse emotions of the rabble.

However, there is no doubt that, bit by bit from the 1830s until the 1890s, one management learned from another how to attract a more demure class of playgoer – though whether this was the result of a conscious desire to lift the tone by excluding the riff-raff or (more likely) the urge to increase profits by bringing in a more moneyed clientele is largely immaterial.

Providing more comfortable seating was one way of attracting a more discerning audience: the pit was notoriously uncomfortable, with wooden seats often with no backs. In the 1830s, for example, Madame Vestris re-upholstered the Olympic Theatre in the Strand (originally an off-shoot of Astley's Amphitheatre) and drew a fashionable crowd to watch burletta – musical plays, usually in rhyme – in which she showed off her figure, playing male roles in breeches.

Putting on the type of play that would appeal specifically to middle-class audiences was another way of changing the mix of the audience. There were partially successful attempts to attract the 'quality' to Covent Garden and Drury Lane in the 1830s, with seasons of Shakespeare, but the vast size of these theatres after both were re-built in the early 1800s made it hard for them to survive financially without stooping to cater for popular taste. But the most notable episodes in the story of the reform of Victorian theatre and the creation of a new kind of West End ambiance took place away from the fashionable centre.

The first of these was the management of Sadler's Wells Theatre by Samuel Phelps, a former Drury Lane actor, from 1844 to 1862. Now thought of as the home of ballet, Sadler's Wells has a very long history. It began as a pleasure garden in Islington next to the head of the New River, an artificial waterway completed in the early seventeenth century which supplied much of the City's water. The Wells were, in effect, an out-of-town spa, for Islington was on the edge of London. A number of theatres have been built on the site, and in the 1840s Sadler's Wells was a typical local playhouse. Charles Dickens recalled a visit there in 1841, and was not impressed by the audience, which he described in a letter written ten years later:

As ruffianly an audience as London could shake together. It was a bear-garden, resounding with foul language, oaths, cat-calls, shrieks, yells, blasphemy, obscenity; a truly diabolical clamour. Fights took place anywhere at any period of the performance.

ABOVE: *A satirical but not entirely unrealistic vision of the pit audience as it was from the late eighteenth to the early nineteenth century. In most theatres the whole floor of the house was filled with rough wooden benches on to which the pit audience crammed together in a noisy huddle more like football fans than modern theatregoers.*

ABOVE: *Madame Vestris as Apollo, one of the male rôles in which she specialized. A fashionable star of the mid-nineteenth century, she was also an actress-manager who wooed middle class audiences back to the theatre.*

Ten years later, under the management of Samuel Phelps, the atmosphere of the theatre had changed entirely. Henry Morley, writing in *Journal of London Playgoers (1851–1866)*, described the pit and the gallery in 1853:

There sit the working classes in a happy crowd, as orderly and reverent as if they were in church, and yet as unrestrained in their enjoyment as if listening to stories told them by their own firesides. A Midsummer Night's Dream abounds in the most delicate passages of Shakespeare's verse; the Sadler's Wells pit has a keen enjoyment of them, and the pit and the gallery were crowded to the furthest wall on Saturday night with a most earnest audience, among whom many a subdued hush arose, not during but just before the delivery of the most charming passages. If the crowd at Drury Lane is a gross discredit to public taste, the crowd at Sadler's Wells more than neutralize any ill opinion that may on that score be formed by playgoers.

Exactly what the audiences were like and where they came from at Sadler's Wells theatre during Phelps's management is very poorly documented. It is known that fashionable playgoers were attracted to Sadler's Wells by the standards of production there and that by 1847 Phelps was selling tickets for his plays in New Bond Street. In his first months of management Phelps would personally throw unruly playgoers out of his theatre, and later would quiet them down so that his drama could be appreciated. Once his audience had changed this was, presumably, no longer necessary as his theatre became less a local venue attracting a wide cross-section of the population, and more a West End outpost. By the 1850s Sadler's Wells was much written about in newspapers and attracted a discerning literary audience, including Charles Dickens, to its Shakespeare seasons.

What happened at Sadler's Wells in this period was, in fact, a reflection of a very general change in London entertainment. Firstly, it was no coincidence that Phelps went into management in Islington when he did for this was the year following the Theatre Regulation Act of 1843, which had broken the monopoly on legitimate drama held by the West End theatres. In his advertising, Phelps stressed that this now meant that London's suburbs could have proper theatres. At the same time the horse-bus services were growing rapidly, and after their great popularity and success during the Great Exhibition of 1851 they linked many inner suburbs like Islington with the West End. The

ABOVE: *A playbill from Sadler's Wells during the reforming management of the actor Samuel Phelps. It was still the practice at this time to present more than one play in an evening's entertainment, sandwiching Shakespeare amongst melodrama and other productions.*

LEFT: *Samuel Phelps, who introduced a run of Shakespeare's plays to the formerly rough-house theatre, Sadler's Wells, in the role of Hamlet.*

man or woman on the omnibus in those days was relatively well-do-do – the mass of the population walked until the introduction of the cheaper horse-tram and 'workmen's fares' on the trains – though a cut below the élite carriage-owning class.

The nature of the audience was determined largely by the starting time of the performance. Productions at Sadler's Wells started at 6.30 pm and were thus suited to a more leisured class, for this was too

ABOVE: *One of London's long-vanished early music halls, Deacon's, which was demolished when Rosebery Avenue was built in the 1890s. It stood in Myddleton Way opposite Sadler's Wells Theatre. Opened in 1861, it provided a rival attraction to the theatrical productions of the Wells.*

early for most working people; but a new audience was allowed in at half price – usually to the gallery, the cheapest part of the house – to see the final part of the entertainment. The Shakespeare productions were sandwiched between popular contemporary dramas; only later was an evening's entertainment reduced to a single play.

The Theatre Regulation Act of 1843 had other unintended consequences: as mentioned earlier, it had the effect of dividing popular entertainment into two, because it was not possible to hold both a theatre licence and a local music and dancing licence simultaneously. The law did not decree that. It came about by one of those unfathomable, unwritten rules of the Lord Chamberlain's office.

From the 1850s, when music hall began to take off, many halls sprang up around Sadler's Wells to provide this new kind of entertainment. By the 1860s the more convivial atmosphere of these halls must have drawn away a large part of the working-class audience that once made Sadler's Wells a rowdy theatre filled with the smell of oranges. As John Pick points out in his study of London theatre, *The West End: Mismanagement and Snobbery*:

From 1860, when the Empire opened in the High Street, with a capacity of 1,500, Islington rapidly became a centre of the music hall. In 1861 Deacon's Music Hall, with a capacity of 800, opened in

Myddleton Way. In 1862, the best known of them, Collins' Music Hall, seating 600, opened on Islington Green. Meanwhile the old Alexandra Theatre in Highbury Park was being re-built with a planned capacity of 1,900, and between the larger fish were scattered many smaller fry; 32 public houses in Islington successfully applied for entertainment licenses between 1855 and 1862, and for a period Islington's 'golden mile' rivalled similar areas near the Strand and in Hoxton as an entertainment centre.

As the music halls grew in number and in size, financially much sounder than theatres because they could subsidize their entertainment with money made from the sale of alcohol, they drew away the popular theatre audiences from the West End. The change came piecemeal and the gallery remained a cheap and popular place at many West End theatres, especially for the Christmas pantomimes. But a pattern had been set whereby West End theatres became the province of a middle-class audience which evolved new and much more refined kinds of behaviour, though not necessarily very refined in its taste or deeply interested in what went on on stage.

Out of the Dusthole

The break between music hall and theatre had been made, but theatre management is a precarious business and it took inspiration and daring to set out deliberately to change the nature of theatre and audience behaviour. As with Phelps at Sadler's Wells, the revolution was begun not in the established theatres of the West End but on the outskirts of theatreland where the rents were much lower and the risks smaller.

In the 1860s, in Tottenham Street which runs off Charlotte Street in W.1, was a typical local theatre called the Queen's, and known locally as the 'Dusthole' – just as cheap, shoddy cinemas were later known as 'fleapits' or 'bug-hutches'. It was in this unlikely place that the West End revolution began. Marie Wilton, a successful actress who had made her name playing in burlesque, the forerunner of musical comedy, decided in 1865 to go into management, with a partner H.J. Byron. She had borrowed £1,000 from her brother-in-law, but could not afford to venture into the West End proper.

She was told the Queen's Theatre was to let. Many years earlier it had been quite a smart theatre but had gone steadily downhill. In her memoirs *Mr and Mrs Bancroft on and off the Stage* (she married an

RIGHT: *At Christmas time in the 1870s something of the boisterous audience of earlier theatre could be found packing the gallery of Drury Lane Theatre for the annual pantomime.*

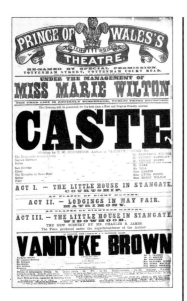

ABOVE: *A playbill of historic importance: the Prince of Wales theatre in Tottenham Street, off Charlotte Street, W.1 was the model for future West End theatres under the management of Marie Wilton. It had formerly been a local rough-house theatre called the Queen's, known locally as the Dusthole.*

actor, Squire Bancroft, who joined her in management), Marie Wilton recalled the reaction of friends when they heard she might take the Dusthole:

> *I was implored by everyone I consulted to reflect before entering upon such an enterprise. 'The neighbourhood was awful', 'The distance too great from the fashionable world' and 'Nothing would ever make it a high-class theatre.' People shrugged their shoulders, and I could see that failure was foretold in every feature.*

Marie Wilton, however, was not put off and began to plot her gentrification of the Dusthole. Her playwright partner Byron wrote to the Lord Chamberlain's office to ask permission to re-name the theatre the Prince of Wales, and the Prince duly agreed. While the old Queen's was still running, Wilton, Byron and his wife went to take a look, and were reminded that the Dusthole was in need of much more than a new name if it was to attract a fashionable audience. She recalled the experience:

> *Mr and Mrs Byron and myself occupied a private box, and saw the performance. It was a well-conducted, clean little house, but oh, the audience! My heart sank. Some of the occupants of the stalls (the price of the admission was, I think, a shilling) were engaged between acts in devouring oranges (their faces being buried in them) and drinking ginger-beer. Babies were being rocked to sleep, or smacked to be quiet, which proceeding, in many cases, had an opposite effect!*
>
> *A woman looked up to our box, and seeing us staring aghast, with, I suppose, an expression of horror upon my face, first of all 'took a sight' at us, and then shouted, 'Now then, you three stuck-up ones, come out o'that, or I'll send this 'ere orange at your 'eds'. Mr Byron went to the back of the box and laughed until we thought he would be ill. He said that my face was a study. 'Oh, Byron!' I exclaimed, 'do you think that people from the West End will ever come into those seats?' 'No,' he replied, 'not those seats.' Of course, he made jokes the whole evening. One woman in the stalls called out to another, 'I say Mrs Grove, 'ere's one for you' at the same moment throwing a big orange, upon which Mr Byron remarked, 'nice woman, Mrs Grove, Orange Grove . . .'*

In a month, with her £1,000, Marie Wilton transformed the little theatre. She had quite a following among fashionable theatregoers,

BELOW: *A satirical view of the impact of the Bancroft revolution on London's West End theatres. Squire Bancroft is snuffing out popular enthusiasm for theatre, and the orange seller is fleeing.*

RIGHT: *A wonderful picture of the tone and style of the Bancroft management on the occasion of their retirement in 1885. They had transformed the Haymarket Theatre into a fashionable place for the upper crust, and had done very well financially. It was the beginning of the end of popular theatre in London's West End and its transformation into a middle-class form of entertainment.*

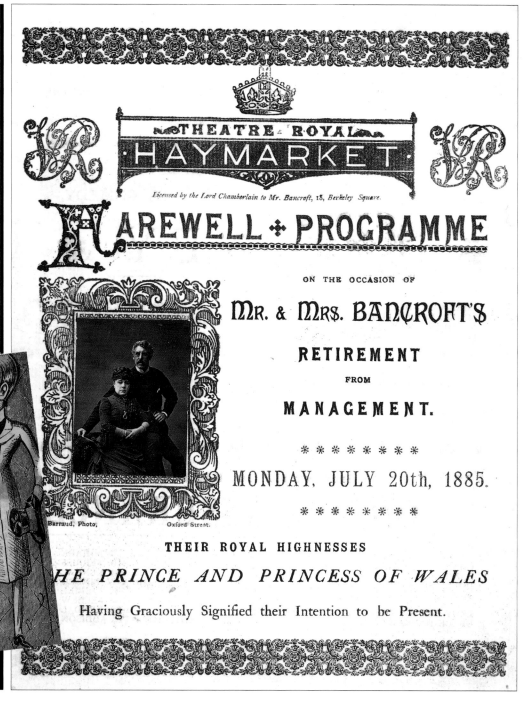

THEATRE ROYAL HAYMARKET

Licensed by the Lord Chamberlain to Mr. Bancroft, 18, Berkeley Square.

FAREWELL + PROGRAMME

ON THE OCCASION OF

MR. & MRS. BANCROFT'S

RETIREMENT

FROM

MANAGEMENT.

* * * * * * *

MONDAY, JULY 20th, 1885.

* * * * * * *

THEIR ROYAL HIGHNESSES

THE PRINCE AND PRINCESS OF WALES

Having Graciously Signified their Intention to be Present.

Barraud, Photo, Oxford Street.

and was confident that at least for her opening they would support her. But it was a time of tremendous fear and excitement:

The hour for launching the little ship arrived; of course there was a great crowd outside the theatre, and the inhabitants of Tottenham Street had, doubtless, never seen such a display of carriages before. The public, who were anxiously waiting for the doors to open, little knew that, but five minutes before they entered, I was standing on a high stool in a private box nailing up the last lace curtain. The house looked very pretty, and, although everything was done inexpensively, had a bright and bonnie appearance, and I felt proud of it. Curtains, carpets, in fact all the appointments, were of the cheapest kind, but in good taste. The stalls were also blue, with white lace antimacassars over the seats. This was the first time such things had ever been seen in a theatre.

The Prince of Wales was a great success, profitable from the first night, and in a short time one of the most fashionable theatres in London. Local playgoers were excluded by the high price of the stalls, up to seven and then ten shillings; by the restriction of the entertainment in time to a single play; by the nature of the entertainment itself which took a comical look at society manners and became known as 'tea-cup and saucer' theatre for its realistic recreations of refined life on stage. The half-price admission was abandoned. It was not long before Marie Wilton had turned the table on the orange sellers. After the triumphant first night she recalled, 'When I was leaving the theatre to go home, there was a woman with a basket of oranges still standing outside, who, when she saw me, exclaimed "Well, if these are your hariostocrats, give me the roughs, for I've only took fourpence".'

The Bancroft era is recognized as the turning point in the creation of West End theatre. In 1880, they moved into the West End, taking over the Haymarket, and causing a storm by reducing the size of its famous pit and putting in expensive stall seats. When the Haymarket reopened, Squire Bancroft had to come on stage to argue his case. The 'pitites' had been put into a lower circle and were shouting, 'Where's the pit?', their demonstration holding up the production. Bancroft boldly talked them down, saying he needed the extra income from the higher priced stalls, and eventually the performance continued.

The Bancrofts' strategy was to make their money from a relatively small, wealthy audience, and not to compete in mass popular entertainment. It worked, for they retired in the late 1880s with a small

ABOVE: *In music halls eating and drinking were as important as the entertainment in the early days, as this sketch of an unidentified London hall in 1873 clearly shows.*

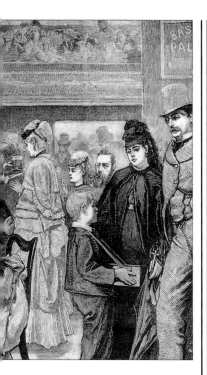

fortune of £120,000. They also, by associating with respectable, society audience, raised their own status, and to a considerable extent that of their actors and actresses, who were well paid. Even before their move to the Haymarket they had their imitators, and when a new phase of theatre building began in the 1860s the style was set for relatively small, smart auditoria, with high prices and little or no room for the orange-chewing vulgar.

Art and the appetite

Square Bancroft was anxious to argue always that he was, above all, a businessman, and his re-styling of theatres was inspired primarily by the desire to make a profit. Indeed, the question of finance underlay much of the rivalry between theatres and music halls from the 1860s; and the issue of competition between them, and how people should be allowed to behave in them, was the chief subject of the 1892 Select Committee on Theatres and Places of Entertainment. This contains some of the choicest and most revealing statements about how the two forms of entertainment were viewed, and why it was thought different rules on audience behaviour should apply in them.

Central to the debate was whether or not music halls should be allowed to put on dramatic sketches. By this time, many of them did; and the theatre managers complained frequently that this was unfair competition. A music hall was always liable to prosecution if a sketch seemed to develop into drama. When a sketch became a drama was much debated, and in time the rules were changed to allow these, so long as they did not exceed forty minutes.

In their evidence to the Select Committee of 1892, the theatrical lobbyists argued that drama was Art with a capital A and that it could not be appreciated by an audience which drank and smoked in the auditorium. Others asked: 'Why not?' and the music hall contingent saw no reason why their audiences should be denied drama.

One of the witnesses was William Bailey, then manager of the Alhambra in Leicester Square, the celebrated music hall. He agreed in cross-examination that dramatic sketches in music halls might reduce the amount of drinking, giving an instance of a little drama he had written himself:

I, as a budding author, then stood looking on very anxious to know how it was going with the audience. The audience were packed up so close that I could not see my own production, but I listened to the applause and felt elevated; but I heard a remark from a lady behind the bar which did not tend to elevate me. She said, 'there is nothing in this; this is a blooming frost' (a frost in music hall language means a failure; it is a stage term). I was rather aghast, because I was congratulating myself upon the success of the sketch. She explained her meaning by saying, 'I have not served a drink the whole time it has been on', and it was the fact.

Clement Scott, the theatre critic, in his statement argued that everywhere, in both theatres and music halls, popular taste had improved and that the division between the two types of venue in terms of smoking and drinking and the right to perform drama was an unnecessary restriction.

Begin, I say, at the right end, if you would lead the people out of the dull and hopeless desert that ends in the drink shop. Allow them to be happy, and do not drive them to despair. If they cannot afford the luxury of a high-class theatre, do not deny them the good and wholesome influence of a dramatic sketch, an honest song, a little opera, a tale of heroism dramatically told. Do not put out the poor man's pipe, when by means of dramatic action and good dialogue, he is told how the policeman saves the life of the despairing woman who would fling herself into the Thames; how the fireman risks his life as bravely as any soldier or sailor in the land.

The theatre managers, like Henry Irving, who were fearful that they would lose their audience if rival theatres were allowed to permit drinking and smoking in the auditorium, were being too timid, Clement Scott argued. At the Lyceum, Irving was a great success with his up-market, smoke-free auditorium. 'Why did he fear competition? If the West End managers want art with a big "A", why not let them have it, but why deny to the toilers and the masses art with a small "a".'

And those who argued that theatre could not be properly enjoyed where smoking and drinking were allowed were directed by Scott to the great playhouses of the East End and Lambeth:

... is there no smoking in the auditorium of East End and transpontine theatres? Of course there is. Placards are put up, 'No smoking allowed', but have you never seen a pipe ablaze in the pit and gallery of cheap theatres? If you doubt my word, ask the police. It is nonsense to say that there is any vast difference between the cheap theatres and the cheap music hall in the matter of smoking

ABOVE: *A scene from the Middlesex Music Hall, Drury Lane, in 1890. Fixed seating has replaced chairs and tables, but there is still drinking in the auditorium, which was not allowed in theatres.*

and drinking. I believe the establishment of free trade in amusements would improve public morals, and would not degrade art in the least.

Though they were supposed to abide by the same rules as West End theatres, the great working-class playhouses such as the Britannia, Hoxton, had a completely different atmosphere. An account of the Brit in its last days is given by John M. East in *'Neath the Mask*. His grandfather was manager of that theatre in 1904, and in the 1960s John East collected personal reminiscences of actors who had played in the theatre. This is his distilled account of Saturday night at the Brit around 1904:

The prevailing smell suggested a subtle blending of orange-peel, human perspiration, greasepaint, dust and pregnant woman. The refreshments on sale included coram populo, thick boiled-beef sandwiches, tail and middle fish, hot saveloys and hot pies and peas. These provisions were handed round by shouting attendants staggering under the weight of their huge trays. The hot pies and peas were contained in an iron canister about the size of an ordinary mop bucket, beneath which was a lighted spirit lamp, to keep the contents hot. Two women followed at a discreet distance. Their function was to carry a small vat of gravy. When anybody purchased a twopenny pie and proceeded to bite a piece of it, the gravy-vendor stepped forward briskly, and poured some gravy into the cavity left by the customer.

Liquid refreshment was equally well organised. Draught beer was pumped up by strong-armed barmen at long pewter-covered counters. All round the auditorium were short-sleeved beer-bearers. Some carried the precious fluid in pewter pots, but that was a refinement reserved for the stall patrons. The pit and the gallery folk were content with the use of cans. Other vendors wore zinc belts round their waist, and these were divided into porter and ale compartments. Each division was provided with a tap, from which the beer-bearer drew off a mug to measure. Not that the temperance playgoer was neglected. Special bars judiciously blended ginger beer and lemonade.

The Lord Chamberlain's inspectors obviously turned a blind eye to the Brit: it was beyond the pale, not part of society, and therefore could be allowed to go its own way. In fact, generally speaking, the change in behaviour in West End theatres had much more to do with social custom

ABOVE: *The painter Walter Sickert's portrait of the gallery of the Old Bedford music hall in Camden Town. Something of the rough-house of early theatre survived in the music halls of the late nineteenth and early twentieth century.*

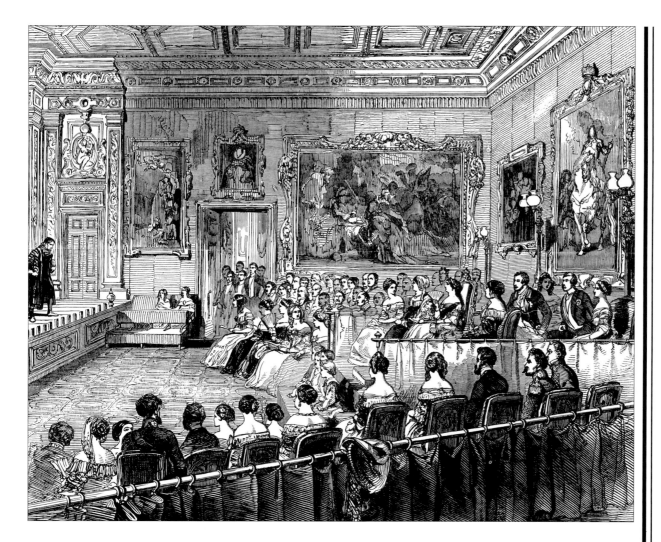

LEFT: *One of the many private theatrical performances commanded at Windsor by Queen Victoria. From her childhood she loved the theatre, her tastes ranging from circus to opera.*

than with any enforcement of rules by authority. What it entailed was the exclusion of the mass audience to make the auditorium safe for Society and – in theory – 'high Art'.

Queen Victoria is amused

One of the great influences of the return of 'Society' to the theatres in the second half of the nineteenth century was the enthusiasm for drama that Queen Victoria showed throughout her life. Her theatre-going is meticulously detailed in her diaries, and *Queen Victoria Goes to the Theatre*, an account based on the diaries by the theatre historian

George Rowell, makes the point that she did a great deal to elevate the status of actors and actresses, and to revive the fashionability of theatre. The celebrated 'We are not amused' is an authentic story from 1884, when Alick Yorker, a groom-in-waiting and Court wit, elicited such a guffaw from a German visitor that Queen Victoria asked him to repeat what he had said. Loyally, he did – a rather risqué joke. The Queen's riposte, according to Rowell, implied not the Royal 'we' but all the ladies present. It was certainly not a general comment on Her Majesty's view of entertainment. Although the Queen never made a public appearance at a theatre after Prince Albert's death in 1861, she had a great many private performances put on both at Windsor and Osborne, in the Isle of Wight, and met all the great actresses and actors, singers and dancers of her day.

The question of behaviour in theatres was really part of this revival of Society's interest in drama, along with its Victorian dislike of mixing with the lower orders and its use of the theatre as a place to meet and parade. Until the 1880s, the auditorium in all theatres remained lit, not darkened, for most of the performance; house lights were dimmed only for some special effect. When the darkening of the house was experimented with in staging Wagner's *Ring* cycle in 1892, there were protests. It was not the rule to put out the house lights until after the First World War. Therefore, the well-dressed, Victorian Society audience was not necessarily any more attentive than the more rowdy and responsive working-class audience, for there was a strong tendency for it to take a greater interest in itself than in what was going on on stage.

In 1874, Clement Scott complained in the *Era Almanack* about talkative playgoers, and attributed this lack of attention to the kinds of reforms that had created the new middle-class theatre:

> *... the modern playgoer ... repairs to the theatre during the process of digesting the heaviest meal of the day, and is sulky at the notion of throwing away at the theatre-door a half smoked cigar or hastily-accomplished cigarette ... The change in the dinner hour and the introduction of the stalls we all admire so thoroughly have both something to do with this chattering and magpie annoyance – a scandal which can only be stopped by a vulgar disturbance on the part of the audience or a determined attack instigated by some plucky actor. Nowadays there is no end to this irritating chatter.*

The dimming of the auditorium lights was general in the Twenties and Thirties, inhibiting such behaviour. By that time the theatre had, with the exception of Christmas pantomimes, become an almost exclusively middle-class entertainment. The last and most amusing of eras was brought in by the serving of tea during the interval at theatre matinées, a treat offered in the better class of seats. Often, the tea had not been consumed and cleared away by the time the curtain rose again, and performers were troubled in the otherwise silent and unresponsive auditorium by the clatter of crockery.

Vincent Foley recalls an incident in the Thirties during a performance of *Catherine* at the Phoenix Theatre, in which Marie Tempest was a principal:

> *In those days, they used to have cups of tea during the interval. Either the waitress, the usherette rather, brought them to you or you got them yourself. In the beginning of the second act the curtain went up as usual. To our astonishment back stage, Marie Tempest did not begin her speech; she walked slowly and surely to the footlights, which were in use in those days, and said, 'Ladies and gentlemen, we are quite prepared to wait until you have disposed of your cups and saucers, at which time we will proceed with the play. Thank you very much.' The curtain was brought down, much hectic getting-rid of china in the auditorium, the curtain rose, they applauded Marie for her frankness. There were one or two agonized members of the audience who lasted 21 minutes with a cup in one hand and a saucer in the other. It was very entertaining to the back row . . .*

W. MacQueen Pope in *Ghosts and Greasepaint* makes the point that audiences always wanted to eat whenever they got near a theatre, and he records some memorable moments from matinee performances in the West End:

> *The matinee teas, at all sorts of shows, are an institution. The enjoyment of them by the audience is only equalled by the annoyance they cause to the players. Some unthinking people blame the managements and the refreshment contractors for serving them. If they did not do so, nobody would go to the theatre at all. . . . In* Call it a Day, *Dodie Smith's big success at the Globe Theatre, there was a scene in which an actress described how her big moment at a special matinée had been spoilt by a woman 'in front' who dropped a*

ABOVE: *By the 1880s, most of London's big hotels, like the Berkeley, were providing dinners for middle-class couples who ate out before or after the theatre.*

teatray with a clatter at the crucial moment. . . . When John Barrymore, the great American actor, was playing Hamlet at the Haymarket, the tinkle of the trays was so great that he paused in the middle of the soliloquy and leaping in the air in fury, shouted 'Teatea-tea!' and glared at the audience before resuming his lines. . . . Ivor Novello was more courteous and tactful. At one very large theatre (in the provinces) the clatter of cups and saucers was so terrific that Ivor Novello advanced to the footlights. 'Ladies and gentlemen', he said 'neither Miss Ellis (the actress with him in an intimate scene) nor myself would think for one moment of interfering with your enjoyment of your tea. So we will just sit here quietly for a few minutes and when you have quite finished, we will resume the play.' He and Miss Ellis sat on a stage rock and looked on . . .

Music hall to variety theatre

In the music halls, as in the working-class theatres, in the Victorian period it was expected that the audience would pay attention to the performances they liked, and ignore or shout abuse at those they disliked. Because music hall turns were brief, introduced originally by a chairman who acted as master of ceremonies, the audience could wander in and out in a relaxed atmosphere. Some of the earlier illustrations of music halls show the performer on stage and the crowd below, eating, drinking, smoking and talking, taking no notice at all. To make his or her name, the artist had to grab attention quickly.

Betty Porczyk remembers how, as a youngster, they used to let performers at the Holborn Empire know if they didn't like them:

In the East End all the youngsters used to want to go to the Holborn once a week at least because it was the local thing, and I used to go on a Thursday night. Well people went on a Monday as well as different nights. I used to go on a Thursday and if at one time the particular turn wasn't any good they would send the word round to take a paper. So what we done, we bought either the Star, Standard *or the* Evening News *– whichever one was the most crinkly at the time – and instead of giving them the bird, the first five rows used to open up the paper and crinkle it all up so the turn couldn't be heard and it wasn't taken back to the Holborn any more. They never came on any more . . .*

Gradually, however, as music hall turned into variety theatre and the tables and chairs of the auditorium were replaced by seating, the atmosphere began to change. It became less and less acceptable to arrive or leave during a performance, although it was always possible to go in and out to the bars between turns.

From the 1880s, when a lot of the smaller halls were being closed down, and the variety theatres became the largest entertainment buildings in the West End, they became very like theatres and the grandest of them, notably the Coliseum, were designed to attract a middle-class audience.

To sweeten the air of the smoke-filled auditoria, perfume sprays were used from the 1880s, and it became a standard and much

RIGHT: *The Hackney Empire, built in 1901 by the most celebrated of theatre architects, Frank Matcham, had abandoned the traditional style of the early music hall and was much more like a conventional theatre. It survives today as a modern variety theatre.*

HACKNEY EMPIRE — THEATRE OF VARIETIES

1.

2.

3.

publicized feature of the design of music halls to have a sliding roof which was opened periodically to allow the fug to escape into the night. Such places as the Hackney Empire, recently resurrected as a modern variety theatre and built in 1901 to the design of the great theatre architect Frank Matcham, still have their sliding roofs, though few of them now function.

By the 1890s, the proportion of revenue in the large music halls that came from the sale of food and drink was falling, though it remained much higher than in theatres. And as eating and drinking was taken out of places of entertainment – with the notable exception of such places as the Britannia, Hoxton – so a new social habit of eating out, before or after the show, arose.

The theatre dinner

Earlier in the nineteenth century, well-to-do men dined almost exclusively at the gentlemen's clubs which had been built from the 1820s. It was not the social habit to go out with their wives. By the turn of the century, with the introduction of the Restaurant Dinner, this had changed. In the ninth edition of *The Night Side of London*, which came out in 1902, Robert Machray says:

These Restaurant Dinners are comparatively recent institutions, so to speak, having come into vogue during the last few years, but they have become almost, if not altogether, the greatest feature of the Night Side of London high life. Fashion shifts about a bit amongst the larger restaurants, and there are certain of them more frequented by one smart set than another. But all, or nearly all, the big hotels have restaurants, and some of the smaller, and perhaps a trifle more select, have them too; they cater handsomely for tout le monde *who can pay. So you may dine at Claridge's, or the Carlton, or the Cecil, or the Savoy, or, if you prefer a restaurant pure and simple, at Prince's, the Imperial, the Trocadero, the Criterion, Frascati's and so forth.*

A much cheaper meal at this time could be had in Soho, where the restaurants, almost entirely run by Italians and Frenchmen, provided according to Machray 'amazing value'.

It will pay you very well to spend an evening ... in exploring the Soho restaurants ... [the menu] begins with Hors d'oeuvres variés *– sardines, smoked herring, anchovies, olives, tomato-salad. Then your choice of clear or thick soups – and the soups (Heaven only knows what's in them!) of Soho are simply marvellously excellent. Now follows the fish course, and here alas! the Soho restaurant does not always shine, and this, it may be guessed, is because fish is never cheap in London. Then an entrée, after which comes the 'Farinasse' which is usually maccaroni in one form or another ... And next there is a slice off the fillet or a piece of chicken ... Finally sweets, cheese, fruit. And all for two shillings or eighteenpence!*

LEFT: *The ultimate theatre of varieties, the London Coliseum was built in 1904, just as cinema was beginning to take away some of the variety audience. It survived a difficult period in the inter-war years, was for a time a cinema and is now the largest theatre in London and the home of the English National Opera.*

RIGHT: *The Avondale Hotel in Piccadilly catered for the new fashion for men to dine out with women, rather than at their club. This was a social change which influenced the character of the Edwardian West End.*

The Bohemian atmosphere of Soho set it apart from developments elsewhere in London. Mass catering had begun around the 1870s with the up-market restaurants opened by Felix Spiers and Christopher Pond, a partnership first formed when they both emigrated to Australia in 1853. After ten years in Australia they came back to London, where their first ventures were in catering for exhibitions, at the Agricultural Hall, Islington, for example, and at railway stations – Victoria and Ludgate Hill.

From these successful ventures they moved into the West End proper with a new kind of restaurant building. In 1874 they opened the Criterion in Piccadilly Circus, an enormous and brilliantly tiled hall designed by the architect, Thomas Verity. They planned a music hall in the basement, but decided instead to turn it into a theatre. And when John Hollingshead opened the Gaiety Theatre, Spiers and Pond got the contract for the adjoining restaurant. Such was the objection to combining eating and the light-hearted drama put on at the Gaiety, that Hollingshead was forced to seal off the direct access from the restaurant to the theatre, even though there was no intention that the audience should do anything but dine in the one and enjoy the show in the other. Spiers and Ponds restaurants were designed to make women feel at home, and they led the way in providing the meal out in town for well-to-do couples.

For the less well-off, the public house remained the most widespread watering hole in town, though few made much of the food they provided. Competition came first from the temperance movement, and by 1884 there were 121 'reformed' coffee houses in London, mostly in converted buildings. But the moralists proved to be poor businessmen.

While the temperance coffee houses were short-lived, more commercial enterprises began to serve the needs of those with modest incomes. John Pearce began with a coffee bar in the City in 1880 and expanded to create the British Tea Table Company, serving 70,000 meals a day in 29 restaurants by the end of the century. Lockhart's Cocoa Rooms were another chain providing cheap food and the Ideal Restaurants chain was founded in the 1880s.

Two of the largest chains were founded by food companies: ABC – the Aerated Bread Company – and the most famous, Joe Lyons. In his early days Joe Lyons had sold food outside the Britannia, Hoxton; the first Lyons teashop opened in 1894 and the first of the Corner House restaurants in 1909.

ABOVE: *A detail from a London Transport poster advertizing the attractions of dining out after the theatre.*

All these new eating places were alcohol-free, and it is a measure of the change in social habits that they presented a fierce challenge to the pubs, which responded by doing away with communal bars, and putting in compartments to provide for those who did not want to mingle with the riffraff. Avoiding those whose behaviour might upset you became an obsession. The compartments also made it easier for women to drink in pubs on their own, and gave some privacy to those who were ashamed of their liking for alcohol. But the pub, which had been the founder of so many innovations in nineteenth-century entertainment, had passed its heyday, as music hall and then catering were taken away.

By the time the first purpose-built cinemas appeared just before the First World War, mass catering was established, shows were relatively short, and there does not appear to have been any issue about what food or drink cinemas could offer. From the very beginning, with the small exception of early bioscope showings in pubs, there had been no alcohol in the cinema auditorium, though whether this was because of custom or the law is not clear. Smoking, of course, was allowed and created that characteristic fuggy magic as the beams from the projector caught the whirling tobacco mist like a car headbeam in the fog.

In the days of silent films there could be quite a lot of noise in the auditorium as the audience responded to the drama on the screen, but in the darkened atmosphere concentration was generally intense. Although audiences responded vigorously to the dramatic episodes in silent films, in quieter moments there could often be heard a mumbling as the words of the captions were read out aloud. Albert Radford can remember this, as well as the change brought by the talkies:

In the late twenties and thirties the cinema was a great boon to most people and was probably their only regular entertainment. I can remember that in the 1920s my mother used to go with my grandmother to the cinema. She used to have to read the titles on screen because my grandmother could not either read very well or see very well. It was a great boon when the talkies came in, it enabled her to go to the cinema on her own and see the film. This was in a cinema in Canning Town but it didn't suit everybody because when the talkies came in there were no captions and people that were hard of hearing were at a disadvantage. I do remember in that particular cinema, a gentleman sitting practically in the front row holding an ear trumpet towards the screen . . .

ABOVE: *The Aerated Bread Company – ABC – went into mass catering for those on modest incomes and the meal out became part of the evening's entertainment, when once audiences in theatres and music halls had munched their way through the show.*

ABOVE: *A collection of slides from the archive of the cinema organist Douglas Sharp who played on a circuit in the London suburbs in the late 1930s. The organist played as the cinema opened for the day, accompanied singalongs and variety turns, modulated between the theme music of one feature film and another, and played the national anthem at the end of the evening.*

By the late 1920s, when the first super-cinema were being built and the first of the cinema organs installed, and many cinema stages for variety shows, something of the live theatrical atmosphere returned between the films. In the Thirties and Forties there were the singalongs, with the audience following the words picked out by a bouncing ball on screen. James Viccars recalls matinees at the Plaza Cinema, Watford, when the talkies first came in in 1929:

> *It was a thing in those days to order tea, which I used to look forward to; but also with the tea came the interval and the lights went up, which I didn't look forward to too much because you had to have a singsong, you see. So the tea arrived on a tray with biscuits and/or toasted tea cake, at the same time on the screen came these various numbers with a little ping pong ball which used to hit the words that you had to sing, you see. One I particularly remember was called Constantinople and everybody used to sing 'Constantinople' with the little ball there. 'See you in the c-o-n-s-t-a-n-t-i-n-o-p-l-e, show your pluck and try your luck and sing it loud with me. Constantinople . . .' And everybody used to go hooray and then get on with their tea. But of course me with half a bun in my mouth . . . it was a little tricky.*

From the early nineteenth century, when wave after wave of new places and forms of entertainment evolved, there had been periodic attempts to control the way in which audiences behaved. Though the temperance movement failed in its own efforts to provide alternatives to the pub and the music hall, its job was done for it by each new form of entertainment which drew people away from drink. In the 1930s, it was argued with justification that the time people spent in alcohol-free cinemas was time away from the pub; similarly, the time they spent enjoying a meal served in a Lyons Corner House served by a neat waitress or 'Nippy' was time away from drink.

Finally, in the 1950s, the temperance dream of a world in which people enjoyed their entertainment by their own family hearth was fulfilled by the boom in television ownership. Even here, as we will see, how to behave in front of a television was a dilemma in the early days, and is still liable to divide London's population along class lines. But it spelled the end of the last great era of local entertainment and very soon the super-cinemas, with their restaurants and their mighty Compton and Wurlitzer organs, were in sad decline, their short-lived luxury in tatters.

ABOVE: *Live entertainment interspersed between films was part of the sense of occasion that a night out at the cinema provided for pre-war audiences.*

5

A NIGHT ON THE TOWN

I N *The Night Side of London*, written just after the turn of the century Robert Machray opens his jaunty account of some of the pleasures of the capital after dark with the following description of Piccadilly Circus:

A humming centre, truly enough, Piccadilly Circus is from eleven to one at night – it is the centre of the Night Side of London ... A minute or two after eleven you will 'take your station'... at a point of vantage... For a few minutes the Circus is rather quiet. A bus now and again rumbles up, and interposes itself between you and the Fountain ... A girl of the night, on her prowl for prey, casts a keen glance at you ... And then a few more minutes pass, and the Circus suddenly buzzes with life; it hums like a giant hive. Here are movement, colour, and a babel of sounds! ... As the theatres and music-halls of London empty themselves into the streets, the Circus is full of the flashing and twinkling of the multitudinous lights of hurrying hansoms, of many carriages speeding homeward to supper, of streams of people, men and women, mostly in evening dress, walking along, smiling and gesting, and talking of what they have been to see. ... You catch charming glimpses in the softening electric light of sylph-like forms, pink-flushed happy faces, snowy shoulders half-hidden in lace or chiffon, or cloaks of silk and satin. Diamonds sparkle in My Lady's hair ... for ten minutes or a quarter of an hour, it is as if all the world and his wife and his daughters, his sisters and his cousins and his aunts, drove past you.

This is the classic image of the West End, which, as the metropolis grew in the nineteenth century, took its character not from commerce or industry but from the expenditure of the well-to-do on pleasure.

Loosely defined, the West End is still that scattered district of London which has most of its surviving theatres and a high concentration of cinemas, as well as restaurants and something of the neon-lit bustle at night which suggests an entertainment centre. But it is quite different from the West End of the Victorian era, or the Edwardian period, or the 1930s or even the 1950s. Bit by bit the sense of being 'On the

RIGHT: *A classic night-time view of the West End: the Haymarket with its two theatres facing each other, His (now Her) Majesty's on the right, and the Theatre Royal. This painting by George Hyde Pownall is probably Edwardian.*

Town', part of the milling crowd looking for a music hall seat here, or some kind of show there, parading around the streets and soaking up the glamour, has faded away, so that, although the streets fill with people when cinemas close, the crowd has no coherence.

One of the reasons for this is that, in order to survive financially, most of the theatres with popular shows have booked seats only, and all of these sold out for months ahead. There is not a great deal to come up to town for on spec, as there was even in the 1950s. A vivid recollection of what was on offer then is given by Ken Sephton who arrived in London from Belfast in 1948:

> *I didn't go home one evening a week for at least three years. The highlight was going to the Empire Cinema, Leicester Square, which was enormous, so luxurious, and put on stage shows as well as films. I would have lunch in the Quality Inn in Leicester Square, nip across to the Empire just before one o'clock, which meant I could sit where I liked, which was the front of the stalls. There was an orchestra with 40 or 50 musicians, chorus girls – about 24 of them – ballet, acrobats, with the programme changing once a month. And it cost 12½ pence, which seems incredible now. And when you came out you felt elated, I'd be walking on air practically, I'd go to a cafe for tea, and then in the evening go to the gallery of a theatre, another 12½ pence.*

A familiar sight in the 1950s was the lines of people queuing for the galleries of theatres, which were not bookable – except on the day, and by a quaint system that has completely vanished. If you pass a West End theatre today it may still have, running along the side, a glass canopy, at one end of which is the gallery door. This was to keep the queue dry in wet weather; and to make them more comfortable and to ensure a place in the gallery, there was a man on hand who put out stools. You could hire one of these in the morning, and it would keep your place in the queue until about half an hour before the theatre doors opened.

The queues for West End theatres, and after the 1920s for the new cinemas, attracted the buskers and retained an element of street life reminiscent of the old West End described at the turn of the century by Robert Machray. But this central entertainment district had been constantly evolving as a national and international attraction from the middle of the nineteenth century. Though a special trip 'Up West' – or, as East Enders called it, 'The Other End' – was always there as an exciting possibility for Londoners, the West End's relationship with the rest of the metropolis was loosened as new suburbs grew up miles away and semi-detached London was provided with its own super-cinemas offering luxury and excitement in the local high street.

In fact, from the 1830s when new forms of urban entertainment – the gin palaces, the new theatres, the music halls and later the cinemas – began to arise it was local, rather than West End, entertainment that was most important for the majority of Londoners. The celebrated music halls and variety theatres of the West End, the Alhambra or the Empire in Leicester Square, were patronized chiefly by the well-to-do and the provincial or foreign visitors. But whereas the West End has survived, London's local entertainment centres have been devastated. Fred Hammond remembers West Ham as it was in the 1930s:

I could walk to Poplar; there was, I think, a Grand there, a Pavillion, the Hippodrome and then right on top of me was the Imperial Cinema, the Grand Cinema and the Canning Town Cinema which was known as the Old Grand. Then we could walk to Plaistow where there was a Plaza, I think. Then there was the Green Gate Cinema, the Bowlene, the Carlton, the Endeavour, the East Ham Granada, the Premier all on top. So you see there were eight or nine there and many more within a very short bus ride. I used to go the cinema perhaps on average four times a week and most people would go at least two or three times a week. It was a dream world for people living in ordinary homes with no entertainment except the radio, and they would go out there and see a different world for three hours of luxury and pleasure.

The rise and fall of popular entertainment is driven by many influences: changing tastes, the relative comforts of home, and the inevitability of what was once thrillingly new becoming in time tediously familiar. What is striking in the history of amusements

ABOVE: *The gallery queue, with hired stools which ensured a seat in the theatre, for one of the most spectacular successes the West End has ever seen – the musical* Chu Chin Chow. *It played at His Majesty's theatre for 2,238 performances from 1916. Its record for a long run stood until 1958, when it was overtaken by* The Mousetrap.

in London is how far back the influences of change can be traced. This is especially true in the story of the rise of the West End.

The rise of the West End

As Michael Booth points out in *Theatre in the Victorian Age*, it was in the mid-nineteenth century that a change was first noticeable in the audiences for West End theatres. Before that time, the bill was changed frequently and 100 consecutive nights was considered a long run. The predominantly local audience was not large enough to sustain a production for much longer.

This began to change quite rapidly in the 1860s when longer and longer runs were recorded: the popular melodrama *The Ticket of Leave Man*, for example, had a first run of 407 nights. What these longer runs indicated in the first instance was that the potential audience for West End shows was increasing. Michael Booth notes that around 1850, London's population had reached three million which was large enough to stimulate a long run in the West End. At the same time, the railways were rapidly linking the West End with the provinces and the number of tourists who might take in a show when visiting London was greatly increased.

Quite a number of witnesses to the 1866 Select Committee on Theatrical Licences and Regulations were already linking the longer runs of West End plays to visitors. John Hollingshead had no doubt:

> *I believe that most of the London theatrical audiences are largely composed of country people; the old metropolitan playgoer lives out of town, and does not go so much to the theatre as he used to do; the provincial people come up to town, and fresh audiences are created every night.*

Hollingshead is clearly referring at that period to the West End, not the local London theatre which was still thriving and would rarely see a country visitor.

The potential of London's West End as a tourist centre had first been demonstrated in a spectacular way in 1851 with the staging of the Great Exhibition. The splendid Crystal Palace, erected in Hyde Park and adorned with works of art and industry from all over the world, attracted more than 6,000,000 visitors between May and October.

No such crowds had ever been seen in the capital before, and the Exhibition, coming only three years after the Chartist demonstrations of 1848, had given rise to fears that riot would break out. More

RIGHT: *One of the first signs that the West End was becoming more than a local, London centre of entertainment was the long run of particular plays. The melodrama* The Ticket of Leave Man *ran for more than a year – 407 nights – in the 1860s.*

THE TICKET-OF LEAVE MAN

than one thousand extra police constables were drafted in, and 10,000 troops stationed nearby by the Duke of Wellington, in case of trouble. The fact that such a vast influx of visitors to the centre of town could be coped with, without any serious trouble at all, was a deeply impressive discovery.

It was estimated that in 1851, visitors to London doubled in number on the previous year to around four and a half million, of whom

MEMORIALS OF THE GREAT EXHIBITION.—1851.

No. XXV.
DINNER-TIME AT THE CRYSTAL PALACE.

ABOVE: *The Great Exhibition held in Hyde Park between May and October of 1851 attracted six million visitors, establishing the drawing power of London's West End.*

just under 60,000 were foreigners. This means that roughly one and a half million Londoners visited the Crystal Palace. After the first three weeks of the Exhibition, admission charges varied. During the week were the shilling days, with a record attendance of over 90,000, and on Saturdays the five shilling days when the better-off could enjoy relative quiet. The *Illustrated London News* of 19 July 1851 described the difference:

> On one day, society – on the other, the world. On the one day, the Nave crowded in such fashion as opera corridors and Belgravian saloons are crowded, and the aisles and galleries empty. On the other day, the aisles and galleries crowded, and the Nave a thoroughfare – a street – swarming, bustling, pushing with loud voices and brusque movements; and people who have sharp elbows, and can use them, and who push along as in Fleet Street, or in Cheapside …

This social division by entrance fee was naturally also a class division, and the different classes were attracted by different things: the middle classes, who had paid five shillings, showed greatest interest in furniture and household goods and exotic foreign exhibits, while the artisans on the shilling days were more interested in British industry, especially their own brand of it.

In his book *The West End*, John Pick sees one effect of the experience of the Great Exhibition in Hyde Park as 'hastening the divide between the popular and the artistic'. While the more fashionable theatres, including Sadler's Wells under Samuel Phelps's management, did well from the 1851 crowds, the minor theatres and penny gaffs did not. In fact, there are no records of the impact of the influx of so many people into London on the fortunes of other, commercial entertainments. A great many existing institutions, notably the churches, cashed in on the tourist crowds by charging entrance fees for tours, and such novelties as Wyld's Great Globe went up in Leicester Square. Robert Altick in *The Shows of London*, a wonderful descriptive account of every kind of curiosity the capital has offered as entertainment from 1600 to 1860, puts the 1851 Exhibition year as the peak – 'the year of the most exhibitions London had ever seen'. These included innumerable panoramas, dioramas and the like.

Although there are no figures, it is doubtful that 1851 did anything much for local entertainment, which remained a world apart. Foreign visitors would not venture beyond the West End unless, like one or

ABOVE: *Such was the popularity of the Great Exhibition that there were complaints that other attractions in London and the provinces lost trade. This is the illustrator George Cruikshank's satirical view of what happened to Manchester.*

two Bohemian Londoners with a taste for 'low life', they made a deliberate exploration. The two sectors of London entertainment were already evolving in quite separate ways. Whereas in the East End theatres and those south of the river an evening's performances – for there was always more than the single play – might go on until midnight, by 1866 West End managers were catering for the visiting trade. Edward Tyrrell Smith, then lessee of Astleys and formerly of Drury Lane, the Haymarket, Her Majesty's and the Alhambra, told the Select Committee in that year when questioned about the new phenomenon of the 'long run' in the West End and the influence of visitors coming by rail:

> *The railway adds to it, no doubt; I try to get my theatre over by 11 o'clock; people come up to town on purpose, and they can go back by the 11 o'clock train.*

Other managers, like Buckstone at the Haymarket, said they noticed the provincial and surburban audience moving away to get trains in the evening. It was this same audience that Robert Machray described in the early years of the twentieth century, streaming into Piccadilly Circus at night – smartly dressed, professional, well-to-do. In 1906, Mario Borsa in *The English Stage of Today* noted the arrival of West End audiences at the railway stations:

> *... trains disgorge hundreds and thousands of fair ladies elegantly attired, accompanied by their well-groomed male escorts. Beneath the lofty, massive and gloomy station roof, between the slimy, blackened walls, among the tireless, panting engines ... through the foul, smoky suffocating atmosphere of the station they thread their way – delicate visions of white, pale blue, or pink, in hoods or wraps of Japanese silk, embroidered slippers and fleecy boas, wrapped in their brocaded opera cloaks, beneath which stray glimpses are caught of the lace and chiffon of evening bodices – or they flit, with a fantastic shimmer of pearls and diamonds, with a soft rustle of silks, satins and tulle.*

RIGHT: *London attractions, like the St James's Hall, Piccadilly, which specialized in black minstrel shows, advertised themselves nationwide in the nineteenth century. Provincial visitors were particularly fond of minstrels.*

This was not the only audience that Borsa noted: yet another came to the West End to queue for the pit and the gallery. They had walked or taken the bus, 'a mixed crowd' of small parties and courting couples mostly from the better-off working class, clerks, shopgirls, the new breed of typists, telegraph and telephone girls.

It was from the 1890s, following the reforms of the Bancrofts at the Prince of Wales and the Haymarket, and their imitators, that the term 'West End' became established, synonymous with the smartest and most refined types of entertainment. More and more the huge London 'popular' audience stayed to be entertained in its own territory, making only the occasional foray 'Up West' where seat prices were too expensive for them. At the same time, West End theatre dominated the provinces, going on tour with the London hits.

RIGHT: *Fashionable night clubs were the exclusive playground of gay young things in the Twenties and Thirties, their intimate atmosphere captured here about 1928 by the painter C.R.W. Nevinson.*

BELOW: *A classic image of the West End theatre between the wars where first nights retained a good deal of the atmosphere of the Society playground of the Edwardian era.*

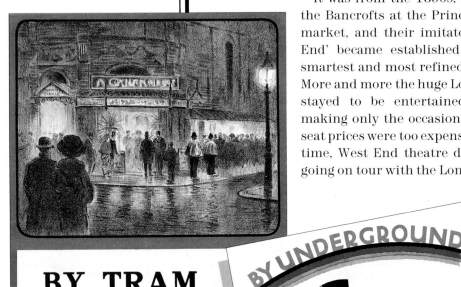

BY TRAM IN COMFORT TO THE THEATRE
ALIGHT AT
SHEPHERDS BUSH GREEN

ABOVE: *The tram provided a cheap form of transport for Londoners either to travel to the West End or to make a shorter trip to local centres, like Shepherd's Bush.*

BY UNDERGROUND

FOR THEATRES, DANCES &

FROM COUNTRY TO THE HEART OF TOWN
30 MINUTES

LEFT: *The Underground Group, private forerunner of London Transport, encouraged the new suburbanites to spend more evenings in town with an elegant series of posters. This one is from 1925.*

During the Great War there was an enormous demand for West End theatre but the audiences had changed, and the atmosphere was never to be quite the same again. In 1920, H. G. Hibbert noted in *A Playgoer's Memories*:

The regular, known, patron of the theatres seemed to disappear. In his place came strangers, constant in mutation – cosmopolitan visitors to town, soldiers home on leave mainly anxious, it seemed, to kill time under any cover and, if they paid any attention to the performance, caring most for inane, vulgar and often indecent revue or crude and unlifelike studies of warfare.

Something of the atmosphere for the pre-war West End as the playground of a smart social set, returned in the 1920s and 1930s, with the élite gathering in the stalls in their uniform of evening dress enjoying light musical comedies for the most part, and the wit of Noel Coward. Most of the big London hotels staged cabaret, and a host of clubs opened with fun names like the Bag of Nails or the Coconut Grove where gay young things could wine, dine, smoke and sometimes dance. As Major Bridgland recalls:

I always used to rather think it was the magic of London, or the magic of the West End. The theatres were great fun. You could dine and dance, which was great fun again, which always meant dressing up. We men always wore black tie and your partner – girlfriend, wife – a long dress; and the great thing you always made certain of was that your partner had a corsage for the evening. And if you felt dashing yourself you might wear a button hole. There were plenty of places to dine and dance, the bigger hotels – Savoy, Dorchester, Barclay, Mayfair – all had restaurants with well known bands, and gave you dinner in the course of the evening, and there would be cabaret. There were the nightclubs like the Coconut Grove, the Bag of Nails, the Kit Kat to name but a few, all much the same with a nice sort of snoozy, low-lit atmosphere. You sat at a table and ordered your drinks, and the exciting thing was you were getting a drink pronto but it was coming from outside because the night club did not have a licence and, in theory, it had been ordered 48 hours before. And you signed a chitty for whisky, gin, brandy, ginger ale or whatever and they rang up one of the off-licence places and a chap would come rushing round on a bicycle with the order and the bottle appeared on the table.

ABOVE: *The cinema came to dominate popular West End entertainment from the Twenties until the 1950s, with day-long shows for which people would queue for hours.*

When you left, your bottle was sealed in your presence by a waiter with your name put on it and it went in a rack. So if you came a week or two months later, your bottle was there and out it came; it hadn't been touched.

When it was all over in the early hours, three or four o'clock in the morning, quite often we used to stop off at a coffee stall at Hyde Park Corner; and it was nothing to see stacks of people in dinner jackets and ladies in long dresses all standing there with a cup of coffee and a hot dog in their hand in the small hours.

Around 1930, a survey was carried out by the London School of Economics and Political Science on the whole social life of the capital, to provide a comparison with a celebrated study undertaken at the turn of the century by the social reformer, Charles Booth. This was *The New Survey of London Life and Labour*. Among many other aspects of metropolitan life, there was an assessment of the way in which amusements and entertainments had changed from the 1890s to the 1930s.

Whereas in Charles Booth's day, cinema was just beginning, by the late 1920s it had become 'easily the most important agency of popular entertainment', according to Sir Hubert Llewellyn Smith, author of the *New Survey*. The latest figures available, for 1931–2, showed that in the County of London (a region smaller than the area then built-up) there were 344,000 seats provided by 258 cinemas. This compared with 94 cinemas seating 55,000 in 1911.

The capacity of cinemas in the Thirties had never been matched by music halls or theatres. Llewellyn Smith's researchers calculated that, with continuous performances lasting nine or more hours a day, the cinemas of the West End and inner London could theoretically accommodate one million people a day – a figure never reached but nevertheless breathtaking in its possibility.

At the same time, the number of music hall and theatre seats had not declined: they had, in fact, risen from 115,000 in 1891 to 142,000. Cinema, it seems, had drawn an entirely new audience. What cinema-going had replaced in everyday life was not certain: it may have simply absorbed the increase in time off – on average, an hour a day since the 1890s – or time that 'was to a large extent passed idly at the public-house, club or street corner'. The social change brought about by the cinema is poorly documented. Yet the Cinematograph Exhibitor's Association estimated that London cinemas had aggregate weekly attendances equivalent to a *third* of the population.

In a way, the film distributors maintained the special position of the West End by putting on the big features there first before 'release' to the locals; and a trip 'Up West' to the Empire, Leicester Square had something of the magic of being 'on the town'.

Suburban Shangri-la

But the most remarkable aspect of the cinema-building boom was the way in which it brought luxury to the suburbs of London, especially when Oscar Deutsch, the Birmingham scrap metal merchant, launched his Odeon circuit with the aim of ringing the capital with cinemas. Though there had been a similar spate of building in the suburbs in the era of the music ball boom, it was on nothing like the scale of the cinemas.

Llewellyn Smith points out in his study that the music halls, or variety theatres, still had a considerable following in the late Twenties and early Thirties, but they 'do not offer such luxurious accommodation as the cinemas, and their programmes are not so long, though their prices (outside the West End) are about the same'. By this time music hall, he says, did not appeal much to the younger generation, and the audiences were predominantly middle-aged, with a majority of men, though 'family parties are more often seen at the halls than at cinemas'.

In contrast it was estimated 70 per cent of the weekly audience at cinemas was girls and women:

> It is no uncommon sight to see women slipping into the cinema for an hour, after they have finished their shopping and before the children come home from school. From six o'clock onwards, the cinemas are largely given over to the younger generation. ... Men tend to go only when they have nothing better to do, or when they have a girl friend to take out.

This was written when the talkie had just arrived, stimulating another boom in cinema-going, and inaugurating the most extraordinary phase in the history of London entertainment, in which a kind of local cinema culture eclipses all else.

The degree to which people lived in the cinema is today almost unbelievable, as is the kind of attention and luxury that was lavished on them. To be greeted within walking distance of home by uniformed attendants and a manager who would usher you in to your favoured seat if you were a regular was truly dream-like. In the afternoons many

ABOVE: *Local cinemas competed for the best promotion of nationally distributed films. Commissionaires with billboards are here advertising James Cagney in* Kiss Tomorrow Goodbye.

BELOW: *Two giant commissionaires – both are 6ft 5in tall – welcoming a page boy to the newly opened Tooting Granada cinema in 1931. Local cinemas in this period had huge numbers of uniformed staff, numbering over 100 in many cases.*

cinemas provided tea with matinees to attract the older folk, housewives and mothers with pre-school age children. In 1938, *World Film News* carried this satirical account of the smarter of two cinemas in Muswell Hill, north London, which it called the 'Mecca of the Aged'. The author is Daphne Hudson:

> *A telling commentary on the nature of the audience is the enormous demand for the deaf aids which are installed. It has even been known for an old lady to request a cushion for her sciatica and accommodation for her pekinese. Retired gentlefolk, a considerable element in the neighbourhood, make the cinema a genteel recreation and choose their films with care...*

As Jeffrey Richards points out in *The Age of the Dream Palace*, the point about this satire is the way it captures the rise of middle-class cinema-going in the suburbs. Nearly every district had, in fact, two classes of cinema: the luxury, slightly more expensive version, and the old and less comfortable 'fleapit' or 'bughutch'. Both, however, provided a weird, smoky, darkened, cosy world into which nearly everyone could afford to escape. Jack Disney remembers meeting his father in the cinema after school:

In the 1930s, living in Forest Gate, our local cinema was the Splendid; and my father, who used to do nightwork, would give me 3d in the morning so I could meet him there. After school I used to go along the outside of the building where all the radiators were, which used to have wire cages to let the fumes out from the gas heaters, and I would go along them shouting, 'Dad, dad' until I got a response; and then when I went in he knew I was there and he would look out for me and wave to me and we would spend the rest of the time watching the film. You didn't have to go in at the start of the programme in those days.

Ivy Groom recalls a local cinema competition in which her winning slogan nicely captures the degree to which the manager thought of his place as a kind of community centre:

It was about 1932 and we had this cinema, the Carlton, which wasn't very big and people were going off it a bit. So they had it altered, made it quite nice, and had steps leading up to the front and a nice foyer inside and a sweet kiosk. But it cost a lot of money so they wanted to try and get an attraction to make it pay, and advertised a competition for a slogan which would draw the crowds. I took this form home and sat up at night making silly rhymes; anyway, I worked it out, 'The Carlton leads with Public Needs'. The prize was twelve weeks of free entrance anywhere in the theatre, and the first night it re-opened it was up in lights, you know: 'The Carlton leads with Public Needs'.

Because so many people were tucked away out of touch with the outside world, it became the practice in some cinemas to project messages on to the screen during the film for members of the audience. Mothers requested that their daughters return home immediately; the crews of ships were told to return to the docks; and when there was a special piece of news, such as the abdication of Edward VIII, it would be projected on a smoked-glass slide.

Despite the overwhelming attraction of the cinema, and the fact that live variety shows as well as films were shown at the larger ones, music hall did not die. The competition most feared by the halls was radio, which had a mass audience by the 1930s. But, as it turned out, radio did not harm the halls much at all: in fact listeners were intrigued to know what their favourite stars looked like, and they could see them at variety theatres. Families and groups of friends still

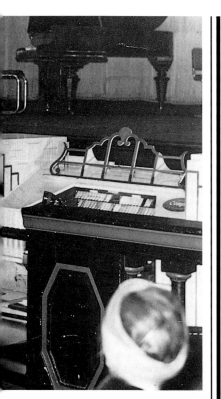

ABOVE: *A scene at the Savoy Cinema, Acton: the organist Molly Forbes presents a prize to a member of the audience.*

kept their regular weekly seats at the local Empire or Hippodrome.

There was so much local entertainment that a trip 'Up West' was hardly necessary – unless you wanted to visit the theatre. As the *New Survey* points out, theatres had almost entirely disappeared from the suburbs of London and, with the exception of the Old Vic and Sadler's Wells, survived only in the centre of town. Because a trip to the West End was so expensive it was a rare and special occasion. Elsie Briars remembers:

> *One of the local people in Enfield, a car hire firm, also could get theatre tickets and one of the people I knew said he could get some; so when we were paid on Saturday we all handed over our shilling a week until we had saved up for these seats and taxi fare. And it was a huge car, I suppose a sort of Daimler, very old-fashioned, and I think there were eight of us packed into this; and we pulled up outside Drury Lane and the doorkeeper had never seen such a huge car, I don't know what he thought was coming, and he hurried to open the door. We were rather tightly packed in and the first one out went out rather unfortunately on his hands and knees and knelt on this very snooty commissionaire's feet while the rest of us got out. But it was a lovely show.*

In the Thirties the West End itself was still worth going to see, even if you did not go to a theatre. Before the days of television, the social life of the well-to-do – fashionable weddings and occasions such as first nights – still drew the crowds as Ethel Hutchings remembers:

> *When my husband and I were courting we used to save up each week, sixpence a week each, so that we could go to the West End and go to the cinema or just go and walk around. We'd go to the cinema and after I'd been to have my knickerbocker glory we would go and watch the people coming down to the theatre, all in their diamonds and pearls; and first nights all these famous people came in all their lovely gowns and fur coats and jewellery, and the men would wear their top hats and tails, and it was really wonderful in those days.*

The pioneers at Ally Pally

Nobody had any inkling that this would all change, the habit of going out for entertainment, when in 1936 the BBC pioneered television, broadcasting to a very small audience from studios in Alexandra

Palace, north London. As a curiosity, John Logie Baird had demonstrated his television system at the Coliseum in 1929. Broadcasts from a rooftop in Long Acre had been transmitted to the stage of the Coliseum, and some cinemas had had similar demonstrations, but nobody appears to have been very impressed.

Jack Disney has vivid memories of the first time he saw television, around 1937:

> *My oldest brother got married, and at the reception my cousin and myself got on everybody's nerves and we were given half a crown to go out and get lost. We had gone to a toy shop and I bought this boat and I was going to sail it on Wanstead Flats boating lake. On the way past the local radio shop, we saw this crowd of people all straining and leaning, looking in the windows, and thought there must be a fight or something going on. Having got right down to the front, we saw what we thought was a cinema inside a shop, and there were dancing girls on this screen. And then the man came to the door and we ran like mad because we thought he was going to go round with a collecting plate for the entertainment.*

Jean Cardy had a very special reason to see the first television broadcasts. Her mother, Louise McBain, was a musician who accompanied marionette shows in programmes in 1937:

> *Nobody had a television in those days except the very wealthy, but a few shops sold them and they would have them in the window displaying the programmes. When my mother was going to be on television my father would find out where there was a shop showing it, and we'd often travel quite a bus journey there and stand in a little crowd in front of the window and all we ever saw was lines and stars because the reception was so dreadful.*

The habit of going out to be entertained – to the cinema, greyhound racing, football – peaked around 1948. After the Second World War, in the years of austerity, people had more money to spend but, because of rationing and continuing shortages, no goods to spend it on. What they could do was go out and enjoy themselves.

In the early 1950s, however, cinema attendance began to fall, probably because too many had been built, and a consumer boom meant that there were other calls on people's income than the box office of the local Gaumont or Odeon. As demand fell, so cinemas began to close; and that in turn gave people less choice and led to further falls

FAR LEFT: *A magnificent orchid corsage for this elegant first night theatregoer at the Adelphi Theatre in 1935. Dressing up for the stalls of West End theatres was the established custom.*

LEFT: *Arrivals for the first night of a Noel Coward play at the Phoenix Theatre in 1936 attract a crowd of onlookers.*

in attendance. At the same time there was a shortage of the most popular American-made films in this period.

But the most obvious cause of the dramatic decline in cinema attendance was the rise of television. Between 1950 and 1959 in the London and South Eastern region, cinema admissions went down by 50 per cent. From the 1960s, cinemas that were considered fantastically luxurious only twenty or thirty years earlier were beginning to close in enormous numbers. By the 1970s, the trappings of the super-cinema – the Wurlitzers and Compton organs, the uniforms and all the other paraphernalia of the dream palace – were museum pieces.

Long before that, the owners of cinemas had been looking for new ways to bring in revenue. Eric Tripp was a Granada manager at the time. He put on skiffle groups on Sundays to bring in young people, which helped maintain the sale of drinks and popcorn. But something more dramatic had to be done if the cinema was not to close:

In the mid-fifties I was asked by head office to go along to a small cinema in Tooting together with another manager and two executives from head office. We spent the entire afternoon playing bingo with the firm's money, not winning anything, and by the end of the afternoon the managers thought it was a load of rubbish and would never catch on. Head office, more concerned with financial gain, thought it was worth a spin.

Bingo, of course, is still going, and though it fulfils nothing like the social function of the old super-cinemas it has saved some of the grandest, such as the Gaumont State in Kilburn and the spectacular Tooting Granada, from demolition.

What has disappeared since television is the fantastic wealth of entertainment which was available *locally* in London. The West End, however, though not half as glamorous as it was in the Edwardian period or even in the Thirties or the Fifties, has survived relatively unscathed.

The greatest resilience has been shown by the theatre. One reason is that the West End theatres had, through their history in the previous century, become aloof from popular entertainment. They were also sustained much more than cinema by a national and international audience which was relatively little affected by television. However, what now sustains successful West End shows and pays the enormous rents of central London theatres is, more than ever before, the long run. At the time of writing, the musical *Cats* at the New London theatre is in its ninth year; *Les Misérables* at the Palace has been running seven years; *Miss Saigon* at Drury Lane three years.

For Londoners the advance booking system means waiting months to see a show, whereas in the 1950s they might have hired a stool in the morning and queued for the gallery at any number of West End theatres. It also means that if they have seen the popular shows they have to wait a long time before any new productions appear, unless their taste is for 'serious' theatre. When foreign visitors stayed away during the Gulf War in 1991 there was, interestingly, only a small fall in the demand for the West End hits: Londoners and provincial visitors took their chance and stepped in to keep the theatres full.

There has, in recent years, been a significant increase in cinema-going, and a noticeable fall in television-viewing. Locally, many small theatres and clubs have opened in the backs of pubs. It might be that a new era is about to begin, in which the advent of the ubiquitous video

ABOVE: *The rise of Odeon cinemas in the 1930s gave every London suburb its new cathedral of the movies in a distinctive, modernistic style. This was the Odeon, Rayners Lane, as it survived in 1979.*

may play a part, releasing devotees of particular programmes from the need to stay in if they are not to miss an episode.

Certainly the way in which people use the television in their homes has been evolving with time. Fred Hammond, who recalled at the start of this chapter his thrice-weekly visits to local cinemas, recalls an early television experience:

My wife and I got married in 1950 and we met some people on our honeymoon who said, 'Come and see us'. So we went over one Sunday evening, and got there about half past seven, and we were determined then TV would not change our lives. When we got there they said, 'Hello, how are you? Sit down'. Off went the lights, television on. This went on till ten o'clock and by the time the show was over it was time for us to go home, so we just got up, said goodbye and never saw them again. Then in 1952 our son was born and that meant not going to the cinema, having to look after a young baby, and we never went to the cinema again till 1972, and we haven't been since, twenty odd years.

Perhaps because the picture was poor, or because watching television was like having a cinema in your home, it was the custom to sit in the darkness in your own living room. It was a habit noted by researchers Rowntree and Lavers in their *English Life and Leisure* of 1951. As an addendum to their observation that people spoiled other's pleasures in the home by having the radio on too loud, they say that television had not yet become an important factor in leisure, but:

Its future development is likely to increase the discomfort caused by selfish listeners. ... For when their homes are equipped with television sets, they will no doubt insist on the light in the room being dimmed for their better enjoyment of the picture. Thus, not only intellectual pursuits such as reading, but also manual ones such as knitting and darning will become impossible.

Prediction is a hazardous business in the field of social behaviour, as it is in entertainment. We now all watch television with the lights on, some knitting and darning their way through the night's entertainment. And television has not destroyed everything around it, as was once feared. While there is no doubt that the great era of the dream palaces is gone for ever, showbusiness survives in new forms. But sadly, today a look at the industry of showbusiness in London is confined chiefly to the theatres of the West End.

ABOVE: *The most spectacular of the super-cinemas, the State, Kilburn, opened in 1937. It is now a bingo hall.*

CHAPTER

6

THE SPIRIT of the LAMP

WEST END ANGELS

I N THE MODERN WORLD of showbusiness, dominated as it is by television, feature films and recorded music, it is a small miracle that the live stage survives at all. It is even more remarkable, whatever the tourist brochures may say about London's 'long theatrical tradition', that the capital's West End should have survived into the late twentieth century to be *the* mecca for playgoers from all over the English-speaking world, rivalled only by Broadway in New York. But it has survived, while other forms of entertainment which arose during the same period – music hall, variety theatre and even cinema – have shrunk to a tiny fraction of their former glory or disappeared altogether.

Such are the mystique and snobbery that still pervade the West End stage that its extraordinary history and, in particular, its finances have remained obscure. The world of theatre ownership, production and management is small, as it always has been, and exclusive. As we shall see, the way in which it operates today is extraordinarily quaint. Always teetering on the verge of collapse, it has been able to pull off some remarkable coups which have made for a handful of successful producers, playwrights, composers and performers spectacular fortunes which would be the envy of any moguls in the modern history of entertainment.

Dramatic bricks and mortar

It is extremely unlikely today that anybody would build a theatre as a commercial venture, yet that is how in the past West End theatreland came about. The motive for building most of them was simply profit, as it was for building almost everything in the Victorian era. No two theatres have the same history, but a colourful account by John Hollingshead of how the Gaiety came to be built in the Strand, with himself as its first manager, shows how the system operated.

In 1866, Hollingshead heard that the site of the failed Strand Music Hall had been taken by someone who was to build a theatre. It turned out the financier was Lionel Lawson, the rich owner of the *Daily Telegraph*. Hollingshead, then stage director of the Alhambra Music Hall,

RIGHT: *By the turn of the century, West End theatre had become divorced from popular London entertainment, and was sustained to a considerable extent by provincial and foreign visitors.*

LEFT: *A scene from a show at the Gaiety Theatre, which attracted a Victorian bohemian set, and was the creation of John Hollingshead's management.*

had been a journalist – he had worked with Charles Dickens – and he knew Lawson. He asked if he could manage the new theatre, the Gaiety, when it was built and was given the tenancy.

Why should a man in Lawson's position, with no theatrical connections, think of building himself a theatre? The answer, according to Hollingshead in *Gaiety Chronicles*, written in 1898, is:

> *There is no pounds, shillings and pence investment known to 'those in the trade' that can equal the building of the right theatre at the right time and in the right place ... theatrical bricks and mortar, far from being a speculation, are something more than what is called a 'dead certainty'. They are, in the language of today, a Klondyke – a living treasure.*

Exaggerated though this assessment is, and though it rests on the assumption that the speculator gets things 'right', it is an indication of how times have changed since theatre building was a worthwhile investment in London. Hollingshead's point is that at the time he took over management of the Gaiety, the tenant took all the risks, and the landlord hardly any. Hollingshead paid his rent three months in advance; he paid all rates, taxes and insurance on the theatre; he gave an undertaking that any scenery, costume, machinery or props taken in for production could not leave without the landlord's permission, and that the theatre should be left as a 'going concern'. He gave a deposit against repairs to the building, and Lawson had the right to two boxes and some other seats when he wanted them.

The Gaiety was, to use Hollingshead's own words, a theatre 'at the right time in the right place'. It was at the eastern end of the Strand, then still the hub of Victorian theatreland, close to both Drury Lane and Covent Garden. In its design and its site it was characteristic of nearly all London theatres. The entrance was on the Strand, a narrow façade giving on to a busy thoroughfare. 'The theatre builder does not want a frontage like a new bank or a new hotel,' Hollingshead wrote. 'He wants access to a chief thoroughfare, if he can get it ... and he can build his temple of the drama on a back stable yard and the storehouses of ashes and vegetable refuse'. In other words, the glittering auditorium, on the outside no more than an ugly brick shell, is built on cheap land, while the front on expensive land is kept narrow.

The cost of building was relatively cheap in the nineteenth century, and in the case of the Gaiety incredibly fast. In fact, the builders were still at work on the opening day, 21 December 1868. As the

ABOVE: *Wyndham's in Charing Cross Road is typical of the theatre building boom of the 1890s. It was squashed into a small site, and seated only 760, many fewer than the former great theatres of the early Victorian period.*

BELOW AND RIGHT: *One of the best accounts of how a Victorian theatre came to be built and managed is provided by John Hollingshead's personal memoirs of the Gaiety, which opened in the Strand in 1868. The theatre no longer exists. Attractive girls in the chorus were one of the great draws at the Gaiety – indeed 'Gaiety Girls' became well known as a quarry for young men of fashion to pursue.*

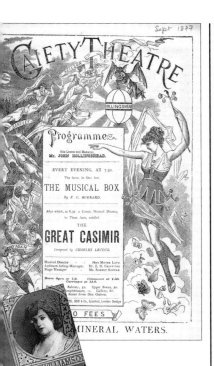

cast went through their final rehearsal, the final touches were put to the building. Hollingshead recalled:

> *About twenty minutes past six the last of the lingering workmen filed out with the implements of their handicraft, leaving a trail of lime-dust behind them. They filed off the stage, but not out of the house, and took up a firm position, with their implements, in the front rows of the upper balcony. When the acting manager remonstrated with them before he opened the various doors to the public, they declined to move, and said they had built the (adjective) theatre and they meant to see it opened.*

Hollingshead let them keep their seats.

As a theatre manager, Hollingshead sailed very close to 'variety' and once called himself a 'licensed dealer in legs, short skirts, French adaptations, Shakespeare, taste and musical glasses'. He was always on the lookout for something new and something titillating. His theatre, its image, its entertainment were all of a piece, a recognizable institution with its own style, which he managed for eighteen years.

Until 1914, nearly all London theatres did in fact have, for long periods under a single management, a recognizable style. You would go to the Gaiety for light relief and the pretty girls, to the Lyceum to be thrilled by Henry Irving, to the Haymarket to be entertained by the Bancrofts, or if you were out in Hoxton in the East End, to the Britannia to enjoy the productions of Sara Lane and her company. Today, West End theatres are simply receptacles for changing productions: they no longer have a permanent individual character.

The Lyceum, under the management of Henry Irving, is a classic case of a Victorian theatre which had a long-established and distinctive reputation. It was not the Lyceum which today stands half derelict and forlorn with its porticoed entrance on to Wellington Street: that was a short-lived variety theatre built on the same site in 1904 as a rival to the Coliseum. Irving's Lyceum had been built in 1834 and had a not particularly successful history before he took charge of it.

Irving had been taken on as the leading man in 1871 by the then manager, a Colonel Bateman who had leased the theatre to promote the careers of his four daughters. Irving was there seven years, and saved Bateman's bacon by producing a play, *The Bells*, which was a smash hit of the time.

In 1878, Irving took over as actor-manager, and ran the Lyceum until 1899. During that time he developed a style of production which

ABOVE: *A cartoon portrait of John Hollingshead, manager of the Gaiety Theatre.*

ABOVE: *Ellen Terry as Lady Macbeth, in one of Henry Irving's lavishly staged productions during his long management of the Lyceum.*

proved to be breath-taking to the Victorian audience. It was not simply Irving's acting that caused a sensation: he was also a meticulous and inventive exploiter of stage lighting and sought to make his profits from lavish productions. In *Victorian Spectacular Theatre 1850–1910*, Michael R. Booth has put together a detailed account of Irving's production of *Faust* in 1885.

The magic of Irving's Lyceum began as soon as the playgoer came into the foyer. H.A. Saintsbury in *We Saw Him Act*, a recollection written in 1939, said:

> *... the spirit gripped you; it had enveloped you before you took your seat, gas-lit candles in their wine-coloured shades glowed softly on the myrtle green and cream and purple with its gilt mouldings and frescoes and medallions by Bartolozzi, the green baize in a diffused bluish mist; the music that did not start but insinuated itself upon you till the baize melted and you were in the picture, beholding, yet part of it.*

Gas limelights, with their intense, rich beam focused by a bull's-eye lens, operated not from the auditorium but from the flies at the side of the stage, blended magical colours, a stage painting supervised in every detail by Irving himself. The limelights were blended with a variety of other lights and co-ordinated in a way which produced breath-taking changes of scene and mood, while the backstage staff hauled hemp ropes and operated bridges and traps in an orchestrated effort that would have dazzled a modern audience, and the orchestra carried the mood, playing continuously through the performance.

Theatre labour was relatively cheap, and Irving's productions required astonishing numbers. For *Faust* he said that 350 men and women were employed, including himself, on stage and behind the scenes. This did not include the orchestra, which was increased from an average of thirty musicians to thirty-six or thirty-seven for *Faust*. Then there was the chorus of eight sopranos, six altos, six tenors and five basses; twenty-five singers in all. In other productions the chorus was even larger.

To increase the effect of his stage lighting, Irving dimmed the lights in the auditorium, then a novel practice, which must have given something of the feel of watching a film in a darkened cinema. His stage-hands invented a machine for producing a steam mist from which Mephistopheles emerged without the steam producing any hiss. Thunder was created by dropping cannon balls on to a one-inch boiler

plate, from where they bounced down a chute: the crack and the rumble. All kinds of subtle stage lighting effects were achieved with battery-operated lamps. Irving himself, as Mephistopheles, had three battery-operated lights fitted in his cap to illuminate his face. Michael Booth believes the colours, from the evidence of contemporary accounts, would have been white, red and blue or green. Some reviewers mentioned a nimbus around Irving's head, a flashing of his eyes, and sometimes a red glow. It is also possible, though not confirmed, that Irving fitted an electric light to the tip of his sword so that when he pointed it at the dying Valentine it lit up the face of the doomed man.

Irving turned the Lyceum into a centre for fashion, entertaining elevated patrons including the Prince of Wales. First nights were sought after, an invitation a great accolade. The most celebrated theatre in London in 1899, the Lyceum was empty and up for sale after 1902, and demolished – except for the surviving portico and the rear wall – in 1904. After he gave up the management in 1899, Irving continued to perform at the theatre with his leading lady, Ellen Terry. But the syndicate that had taken over the Lyceum lost money on all but the Irving seasons, and when the London County Council demanded alterations they could not pay.

The age of the actor-managers in the West End reached its peak when Irving was at his height: there was Beerbohm Tree at His Majesty's Theatre, which he built on the profits he made from the production of Trilby at the Haymarket opposite; Charles Wyndham at Wyndham's, Charles Hawtrey at the Comedy, and so on. They were part of a new and glamorous West End world in which they won respectability for themselves, and to a considerable extent for the theatre, still regarded as socially and morally dubious by older Victorians. Irving was the first actor to be knighted, in 1895: from that time on it has been a convention that the leading actors and actresses of the day should be recognized in the honours list. West End theatre also had a national dominance, with companies touring the provinces by train, their scenery and costumes hauled in up to eight freight cars.

But the Great War put an end to the era of the actor-manager. West End theatres went over to musicals and frivolous and bawdy entertainment, and by the time the war was over most of the old actor-managers were long retired, or had died. In an account of the life of Sir George Alexander, the manager at the St James's Theatre (demolished in 1957), A. E. W. Mason, writing in 1935, noted the difference between the atmosphere before and after the Great War:

TOP LEFT: *The celebrated witches' kitchen scene from Irving's production of* Faust *at the Lyceum, in which he used a dazzling array of lighting effects.* BOTTOM LEFT: *A poster for* Faust, *which was extremely costly but a huge success, netting Henry Irving around £250,000 at the box office in London and on tour.*

ABOVE: *Herbert Beerbohm*
Tree, one of the great actor-
managers of the Victorian
period, in his famous role as
Svengali in the play Trilby,
which made him so much
money at the Haymarket
that he was able to open the
new Her Majesty's Theatre
opposite in 1897.

A first night at a theatre in the year 1900 was an event in the social
life of the town. There are too many of them in 1935 to arouse more
than a languid interest ... Also there are too few men and women
acting in their own theatres. The theatre is now accommodation for
a play. In 1900 it was that and a good deal more. It was definitely
associated with someone, an old friend as it were, who for good or ill
had chosen the play which the audience was now to see, who would
himself or herself shortly appear upon the boards. It was more vital
on that account. It was less of a lodging-house. There was a thrill in
the air as the auditorium filled. Would the old firm do it again?

The challenge of the super-cinema

Whereas in its heyday in the 1890s, West End theatre had felt threa-
tened by the challenge of music hall, which was making great profits
from a popular audience and building on a larger scale than the
theatre, the challenge it faced between the wars was even greater. In
the 1920s, as the first super-cinemas went up in Leicester Square and
other parts of the West End, the theatres dissociated themselves from
this new form of entertainment, which was considered vulgar. In
1908 a Society of West End Managers had been formed to protect
theatre's interests; and SWET, as it became known, resisted any ad-
vances from film companies to show stage plays. Even when the talkies came in in 1928, the stars of the screen were not considered to be
actors and actresses, though very soon the high salaries offered by
film companies lured stage actors away from the theatre.

The survival of West End theatre during the pre-eminence of cinema
is, in retrospect, quite remarkable and might be seen as a benign effect
of its determined exclusiveness and snobbery, much criticized by
John Pick. By staying aloof from mass entertainment and insisting on
the social and artistic superiority of live theatre over celluloid drama,
SWET perhaps sustained the special appeal of the stage. The fact that
the West End audience included a large number of tourists must also
have helped sustain the theatre, for cinema existed all over the world
whereas a night at a London show was a special experience.

But the inter-war years were hard times for London's most vener-
able playhouses. Covent Garden, which because of its size had always
found it hard to make ends meet, survived in the Twenties between its
unprofitable opera seasons, managed and sponsored by Thomas Bee-
cham, by leasing its grand auditorium for ballroom dancing, film
shows, cabaret, circuses and pantomime. By tradition in the large

London theatres, pantomime had been the financial saviour – a resort to popular entertainment for a season at Christmas time to subsidize less lucrative productions during the rest of the year. When music hall was in the ascendant Augustus Harris, manager of Drury Lane, had had the idea of bringing in variety stars to swell the box office for the Christmas pantomime.

His first venture in 1880 was *Mother Goose and the Enchanted Beauty*, which starred Kate Stanley from the Alhambra and Arthur Roberts, a music hall comedian. These spectacular productions – *Sinbad the Sailor* in 1882 had 650 performers on stage at one time for its procession of the thirty-six Kings of England and their retinues – were costly, but reaped rich rewards.

In the 1930s the future of Covent Garden was very much in doubt. Its position in the midst of London's fruit and vegetable market did not help and it looked at one point as if it would be demolished. At the outbreak of war in 1939 it was saved when Mecca took it over as a dance hall for the troops.

Since the Twenties it had been possible to convert it into a huge ballroom by covering the stall seats with boards. The band played in the centre. There are those who remember it well. Hilda Forrest met her future husband at a Covent Garden dance in the 1930s:

It was absolutely beautiful, it was fairy land. There was Herman de Luski and his orchestra in the centre, and we danced around the band on a sprung floor. This little Scots chappie came down from the gallery and whisked me off for a quickstep and asked me to have coffee with him, and he became my husband.

In effect, ballet and opera were subsidized by more popular forms of amusement at Covent Garden before the last war. It was during the war, when a groundswell of opinion favoured 'reconstruction' in times of peace, the idea of the National Health Service was forged and the modern welfare state took shape, that, for the first time, the idea that the State should come to the aid of the Arts arose.

While servicemen quick-stepped around the floor at Covent Garden, Drury Lane became headquarters of ENSA, acronym for the Entertainments National Service Association. This was a morale booster for the troops, whether stationed in Britain or abroad. Sponsored by the Government, by the end of the war it had cost £14 million, employed an estimated 80 per cent of British actors at some time or other, and played to a total audience of 500 million. ENSA, under the director-

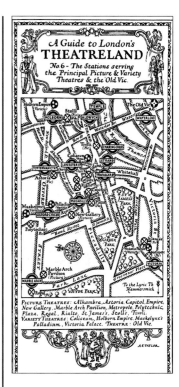

ABOVE: *A guide to popular West End theatreland, as seen by the promoters of the London Underground group, commercial forerunner of London Transport. By the 1930s, the 'picture theatres' outnumbered the variety theatres, and attracted a vastly greater audience than 'conventional' theatre.*

ABOVE: *In the late nineteenth century, Drury Lane became famous for its annual pantomime, which might run for months, and include the top music hall stars. Other West End theatres, however, did not mount this very lucrative kind of production: they were too small, too intent on keeping 'long runs' and committed to an audience more exclusive than that attracted to pantomime.*

ship of Basil Dean, put on popular shows as well as introducing a large number of servicemen and women to 'straight' theatre for the first time.

On the home front, a much smaller organization, CEMA – the Council for the Encouragement of Music and the Arts – was set up by a charity named the Pilgrim Trust, with additional money provided by the Treasury. CEMA was much more exclusively 'arty' than ENSA, bringing classical music to wartime factories, a cultural caravan for the corps of civilians.

Though CEMA made much of its supposed discovery of a hidden appetite amongst the toiling masses for high culture, it was not always well received. Elsie Briars recalls a visit to the factory where she was a welfare worker:

CEMA came once a month, but they were very highbrow: our people weren't very receptive to it, and we often had empty rows of seats ... Sometimes they used to wait till the artists left the stage before they put the lights on, so that they could not see it was empty. But I remember on one occasion when four horrible little boys just about fourteen years old, just left school, stayed glued to their seats in the front row. I found out when I enquired that the cellist had her skirt caught up on the cello and they had been able to see her suspenders, and it kept them enthralled until I fetched them out.

After the war there was anticipation that the Government would continue its sponsorship of the Arts through some peace-time organization. But when, in 1945, the economist John Maynard Keynes, by then Lord Keynes, announced the creation of the Arts Council, with himself as the first chairman, it was fashioned not out of ENSA but out of CEMA. In other words, despite the rhetoric with which the Council was launched in which Keynes said he would like Merrie England's regions to be merry in their own way, the Council took a 'highbrow' view of art.

An immediate beneficiary was the ailing Royal Opera House, Covent Garden which, after its wartime ballroom days, had been taken over by a new syndicate anxious to keep it going. The Arts Council subsidy was not great in the early days, but gradually Covent Garden and the prestige arts – opera, ballet and Shakespeare – took the lion's share of government funding.

Today, out of total Arts Council funds of just over £220 million, the Royal Opera House, with its three companies, the Royal Opera, Royal

Ballet and Birmingham Royal Ballet, takes nearly £19 million annually. In the early 1980s the Royal Opera House received nearly twice in grant what it raised at the box office; now it nearly matches its annual Arts Council subsidy with box office receipts. It has raised prices of seats more than threefold in the last decade, with an average price now of £45. Yet there is a subsidy of £28 on every seat sold and each performance at Covent Garden is underwritten on average to the tune of £57,000. The Royal National Theatre, built by government funds channelled through the Arts Council, takes nearly £11 million; and the Royal Shakespeare Theatre, based in Stratford-upon-Avon but with a London base at the Barbican, takes over £8 million. The English National Opera, based at the Coliseum – the building has just been bought for the ENO with government funds from the previous owners Stoll-Moss – takes over £11 million. In addition, the London Arts Board gets just over £10 million, more than twice as much as any of the nine other regional arts boards.

It is interesting to compare the position of the two old Patent Theatres, one of which has weathered all the storms as a purely commercial theatre, and the other which has become, in effect, entirely dependent on Government subsidies. While Covent Garden puts on a rich variety of productions, its backstage staff constantly re-seating for a new ballet or opera, Drury Lane, at the time of writing, has been home for three years to the smash hit musical, *Miss Saigon*. Whereas Covent Garden gets a hand-out of £57,000 for each performance, the production company which leases Drury Lane, the hugely successful creation of Cameron MacIntosh, *pays* the freeholder – presently an Australian company – £55,000 a week in rent.

It is interesting, too, that whereas something like two-thirds of West End theatre audiences come from the provinces or abroad, the figures are reversed in the case of opera and dance. For these highbrow entertainments, Londoners make up around two-thirds of the audience, or just under. In contrast, modern musicals, the single most popular kind of show put on in the West End, get 80 per cent of their audience from outside London.

From this raw, statistical portrait it might be inferred that, with the exception of the small band of ballet and opera enthusiasts, London's West End has little to do with Londoners. But this is not true. Those staging commercial shows rely on the capital's theatrical enthusiasts in two critical ways: to provide finance for any new production, and to judge it.

LEFT: *Just after the outbreak of the Boer War, the Drury Lane Christmas pantomime of 1899 is sharply topical.*

The London audience

Although a long-running show like *Cats* will, ultimately, get the bulk of its audience from outside the capital, in its first few weeks it is the local London audience which provides the critical appraisal. The belief is that what showbusiness people call 'word of mouth' – the buzz of approval or disapproval a production gets in its first few weeks – is more important than what the critics say in creating a London success. It is word of mouth which brings in the advance bookings that begin to make a show viable, for musicals can now cost up to £2 million and may take a year to break even. The Broadway audience, in contrast, waits to see critical approval of a production before endorsing its success.

The other way in which a tiny section of the London audience is critical is that it is prepared to invest in new shows, principally in the hope of making a spectacular profit by backing a winner. It is quite remarkable that the bulk of the money for new shows comes from small syndicates or individuals investing a few thousand pounds each. These backers are known in the trade as 'angels'; and though they have always existed in London showbusiness, today they are more important than ever before.

Unfortunately, we do not know who they all are, for the key producers keep restricted lists of 'angels' which are not made public. The general belief is that the majority are Londoners who, for their small stake, can enjoy a seat at the first night of a show and a chance to meet the stars. One such angel is Eddie Jones, who used to be a bookmaker. He was brought up on variety at the Shepherd's Bush Empire where he went once a week with his family, 'first house on Monday night and out for stewed eels afterwards'. As a teenager, however, he became fascinated with the glamour of first nights in the West End.

He first became an angel in 1961 when he saw an advertisement in *Sporting Life* which said 'Showbiz gamble'. It turned out to be the The *Father* by Strindberg, starring Trevor Howard, but it failed. Jones lost his money but not his appetite for the excitement of the gamble and the association with the glamour of the West End. In thirty years of investing in shows he has, like all angels, had many failures and a few successes.

When *Cats* was being put together by Cameron MacIntosh and Andrew Lloyd-Webber – the most formidable West End team today – they found it hard to raise funds. It was at the New London Theatre, which had had a run of failures, and was not on the mental map of

ABOVE: *A scene from* Miss Saigon, *the long-running hit that has occupied Drury Lane theatre for several years. Whereas Covent Garden Opera House is heavily state-subsidized, Drury Lane remains a commercial theatre.*

RIGHT: *One of the greatest successes of the modern West End theatre has been* Cats, *which was funded by a large number of small investors or 'angels', all of whom have been rewarded handsomely for taking a risk on an unlikely show, in an 'out-of-the-way' theatre, the New London in Drury Lane.*

most Londoners and tourists – position is still important for West End theatres. The finances were put together in a large number of very small units of £750 each – Eddie Jones had his stake despite his misgivings about the theatre. According to a new book *Investing in West End Theatrical Productions* by Philippe Carden and Bee Huntley, that small stake in December 1980 was worth £16,125 in profits over the next ten years. Eddie Jones recalls that the fifth-year party for *Cats* had more guests than he had ever seen, so many 'angels' had taken a single unit stake.

Investing in the theatre is one of the riskiest gambles any venture capitalist can take; the compensation is a share in that West End glamour which has proved to be so remarkably tenacious over the years.

The commercial sector of West End Theatre does not, it appears, resent the privileged position of the grant-aided companies which do not have to achieve financial success. These, in an indirect way, support profit-making productions by providing training grounds for singers and dancers, both through the London companies and those outside. It is said, for example, that *Cats* would not have been possible without dancers trained and sustained by the Royal Ballet; and singing and dancing – the talents required for commercial musicals – are the areas most heavily subsidized.

By a strange twist of history, then, London's West End theatre can be said to have survived by clinging to the exclusivity (which has since the war been under-pinned by State subsidy) first awarded by those idealistic, highbrow reformers who dreamed of bringing culture to the masses. They have not, of course, done anything of the sort. The masses, through taxation, have subsidized high art, which few among them appreciate; even today the theatrical audience is predominantly from the 'professional' classes. And yet the London audience, maker and breaker over the years of showbusiness fortunes, retains a theatrical influence on the world stage.

Though London has always had its innovators and its stars, its greatest influence has been as a testing ground and a market place for popular entertainment in the English-speaking world. Since the early nineteenth century London has been the stage on which performers of all kinds have wanted to enthrall. The first great metropolis of the industrial age, London's present-day reputation as the world centre for theatre is a legacy of that golden era. It is still, despite all the bogus talk of its long-standing theatrical tradition, very much 'in the limelight'.

INDEX

Page numbers in *italic* refer to the illustrations

ACKNOWLEDGEMENTS

It would have been quite impossible to compile this book in the short time available without the generous help of a great many people. Special thanks to Michael R. Booth, John Pick, Jan Shepherd, Louis James and George Rowell on the history of theatre, and to David Cheshire, Peter Bailey, Jacky Bratton and John Earl on music hall. Brian Harrison provided a valuable history of drink and pubs, Robert Thorne of restaurants, and Jeffrey Richards and Alan Eyles of cinema. Denis Norden's recollections of his days as a cinema manager were invaluable, as were the memories of all those people who wrote to us in answer to newspaper advertisements. A special word of thanks to Virginia Buswell for her research and support, and to Andy Garrett and Janet Storey for their interviews. For his personal knowledge of London's theatrical past, thanks to Colin Sorensen. Philippa Lewis was as intelligent as ever in her picture research. The London Weekend Television Reference Library was helpful as always, tracking down hundreds of books and articles from many different sources. For their help with illustrations, thanks to the staff of the Mander and Mitchenson Library. My thanks to Carl Thomson and Patrick McDonnell for their dedication which got the television series finished on time, and to Robin Paxton and London Weekend Television for commissioning it. Finally, thanks to Sarah Hoggett of Collins & Brown for her attentive work as editor in difficult circumstances. All errors of fact or interpretation remain, of course, my responsibility.

Picture Credits
Bishopsgate Institute 23; Bodleian Library, Oxford 19 (right); Bridgeman Art Library 11, 19 (left), 22 (right), 135, 147; British Museum 105; Cadbury Ltd 103 (right); Donald Cooper 157; Courtauld Institute of Art, Witt Library 115; E T Archive 18, 41 (left), 45, 51, 58/59, 70, 76/77, 91, 106 (left), 122, 155; Fine Art Photographs 127; Ronald Grant Archive 8, 44 (left), 101, 110 (left), 136/137, 138, 145; Greater London Photo Library 15 (both), 17, 37 (top), 139, 144; Guildhall 20, 31 (right), 123; Hackney Archives Department 27 (right), 121; Hulton Picture Library 31 (left), 32, 34, 43 (right), 60, 61 (right), 63, 87, 88 (left), 89, 93, 95, 100, 112/113, 134/135, 138/139, 142/143; Islington Local History Collections 2, 66 (left), 106 (right), 108 (left); Michael Le Poer Trench 156; London Transport Museum 102, 123, 134 (both), 153; Mander & Mitchenson Theatre Collection 21, 27 (left), 35, 36, 37 (bottom), 38, 39, 40, 42, 46, 47, 49, 50/51, 55, 59 (right), 61, 62, 63, 65, 66 (right), 67, 68, 68/69, 74, 78/79, 83, 84, 94, 96, 96/97, 98, 98/99, 99, 107, 108 (right), 110/111, 111, 129, 131, 133, 135, 146, 148, 149 (both), 150, 151, 152, 154; Mary Evans Picture Library 13 (both), 14, 24/25, 75 (both), 80, 81, 90/91, 92, 96, 103 (left), 104, 109, 116, 119, 124, 132, 132/133; Mansell Collection 48/49, 114/115; Pollocks Toy Museum 52, 54, 56, 57; Ann Ronan Picture Library 53, 72/73; Royal Collection, St James's Palace, by kind permission of Her Majesty the Queen 71; J. Doug Sharp 43 (left), 44/45, 124/125, 125, 141 (right); Sotheby & Co., 26; Stoll Moss Theatre Archives 41, 45, 58, 59, 76/77 (both), 87, 122; The Tate Gallery 150; Victoria & Albert Museum 28, 33.